MAKING CHANGE

MAKING CHANGE

A D.U.I. Treatment Workbook

PHILLIP CHARLES KARPINSKI,
LICENSED THERAPIST

iUniverse, Inc.
Bloomington

MAKING CHANGE
A D.U.I. Treatment Workbook

iUniverse books may be ordered through booksellers or by contacting:

iUniverse
1663 Liberty Drive
Bloomington, IN 47403
www.iuniverse.com
1-800-Authors (1-800-288-4677)

ISBN: 978-1-4620-2403-2 (sc)
ISBN: 9781462024049 (ebk)

Printed in the United States of America

iUniverse rev. date: 07/13/2011

Contents

TESTIMONIAL

MY STORY—ONE ALCOHOLIC'S JOURNEY

From seventeen to some time in my late twenties, my perception of an alcoholic was that of a homeless man in a trench coat carrying a bottle of cheap wine around in a paper bag. I don't know exactly when, but some time in my early to mid-thirties, that perception began to change. I started drinking and using drugs when I was "sweet sixteen." An older friend of mine, a very mature seventeen, had invited me to one of the popular high school kid's party and it was just down the street from my house. We had my oldest brother buy us a pint of Southern Comfort and my first sip was magic. The warmth trickled down my body, knocking out every raw nerve of insecurity and shyness I had felt my whole life. It was like I was alive, really alive, for the first time ever. I finally felt like I belonged, like I could talk to other people, like I fit in. I spent the next twenty-one years chasing after that magical euphoria. Sometimes I thought I had found it again. But more often than not, it would be nights full of black outs, sloppy drunkenness, fights with friends and strangers, driving while beyond intoxicated, and actions that left me full of shame, guilt, and remorse.

Any normal person would have realized that they had a drinking problem and needed to stop when at seventeen-years-old they went outside at a party to get some fresh air after drinking just a little too much vodka, passed out under a car, and got their head partially run over while another party-goer tried to back out to leave. Or while camping out in Joshua Tree, they blacked out in the bed of a truck, then projectile vomited into their boyfriend's face, again after just a little too much vodka. My reasoning at the time—vodka doesn't like me very much and I shouldn't drink it anymore. But beer, Southern Comfort, Bacardi 151, Tequila, whatever, it was all open season. After all, I was just having fun and trying to escape from the miserable home life we had and rebelling against the domination of authority figures and the world at large.

At twenty-five, I ended up marrying someone who drank and partied just like I did. Everything revolved around drinking and partying. The day before I was to graduate from a four-year college, we drank so much I was completely hung-over the next day and practically unable to go through the ceremony. I could not even enjoy the lunch and celebration afterwards with my family. A marriage built on chaos and irresponsibility is bound to fall apart, and mine did. That's when my drinking really took off. And that's when my eyes slowly started to open, as there was no one else there anymore to blame for my miserable existence, my warped emotions, and my demoralizing actions. There was just me.

I continued drinking and partying for several more years, spiraling further and further down into a black abyss.

Over the years, I had tried everything—psychotherapy, depression medications, self-help books—anything to make me feel normal. But nothing worked. I desperately tried to control and enjoy my drinking—taking only a $20 bill to the bar with me, plus a few singles for tips, but later on making sure I threw in an extra $10 "just in case." I usually ended up spending it all, plus getting shooters bought for me by friends. Or I would try to drink beer only and cut myself off from the "shooter bar," but that never seemed to work either. After realizing I was drinking from Thursday, Friday, Saturday, and Sunday, to Monday and even Tuesday, I tried to cut out a night or two here and there. That, too, only worked temporarily. Soon I was buying 12-packs to keep in my refrigerator at home, rationalizing that at least I wasn't going out to the bars. But drinking continued to consume my life—either I was obsessed with thinking about it and planning my next drunk, or I was right there in the middle of it.

On my thirty-seventh birthday celebration at the bar, a night that was supposed to be all about me, but wasn't, I hit my bottom. I don't remember the details, but I do remember the feelings. I felt let down, disappointed, disenchanted, disgusted, angry, and most of all, heart-broken. My best friend at the time even ended up slamming her beer bottle into the middle of my birthday cake. A "friend with benefits" ended up driving me home that night. I cried all the way home and when we got to my apartment, he wiped my tears and offered to come inside. Even though he cared and wanted to help, I sensed what he really wanted and it crushed me even more. I said good-night and went inside to the comfort of my own surroundings where there was no judgment, no ridicule, no arguing, no fighting.

When I awoke the next morning, I knew I couldn't live this way any longer. I called my good friend who I had known since Jr. High School, who I used to drink with. She was sober now and in A.A. She asked me if I wanted to go to a meeting with her. We had done this dance off and on over the past two-and-a-half years, but it never stuck for me. I said sure, as long as it wasn't a Participation Meeting. She picked out a Speaker Meeting on the following Friday night and we drove there in separate cars after sharing dinner together. It was pouring down rain and I was all dressed up in my western wear ready to go two-stepping at the country bar just miles from the meeting. We went inside. Instead of a large Speaker Meeting, we found a small group of recovering alcoholics and realized it was a Participation Meeting, the kind I dreaded. I trembled in fear that I would have to say something. I wanted to leave, to run out the door, but my friend reassured me that it was all okay. I don't know what anyone said that night, but I do remember a man getting up to share who said he had seventeen years, but went out. He was back. He was a Newcomer again. My mind raced. At the end of the evening, we held hands and prayed. In that moment, I felt something. Something I had never felt before. It was a presence, a peace that filled the room. There were no bright lights or sounds or things moving . . . . just an essence. And it filled me. My friend and I stood outside just under the porch, shielding us from the rain, as we said our good-byes. As I drove south on the main boulevard to the freeway, I had no desire to head west towards the bar. But instead, got on the on-ramp heading east and drove directly home.

When I spoke to my friend the next morning, she was shocked to hear that I didn't go to the bar. She was sure I would. So was I, before the start of that meeting. She shared her sense of something, a Power, in that room the night before. Now it was my turn to be shocked, as I thought I was the only one who had felt it. I was embarrassed to bring it up first. I would learn over the years to come that everything I've ever felt, and everything I continue to feel, seems to be a part of my make-up, part of being an alcoholic, and you will always find someone else within these rooms that have felt, or feel, the exact same way. I would also learn later on that my friend was my "Eskimo." That special person who holds the doors of the Program open long enough for you to finally find your way and stay. I am eternally grateful to her for that.

Today, I have twelve-and-a-half years of sobriety. In the beginning, it was all about not drinking and learning how to do things without drinking being a part of my life. But I was to learn soon enough that there is so much more. The obsession to drink left me after about forty-five days. But there I was, stark raving sober and emotionally sixteen-years-old again. I have heard that you stop growing up at the age you were when you began drinking. I found this to be true. I went to meetings three to four times a week, sometimes more, sometimes less. I got a sponsor who began to take me through the Twelve Steps of the Program. I began attending social A.A. functions and events, and took commitments at meetings, which truly kept me sober on more than one occasion. Slowly, over time, I began to learn how to deal with the things and the feelings that I used to drink over. I learned tools to use to substitute for the behavior and habit of drinking. I began to see that alcoholism is so much more than a drinking disease. It is definitely a medical disease to which we have a physical allergy, once consuming alcohol, we cannot stop. Then there is the mental obsession where it consumes our every thought and we plan and scheme and lie, cheat, and steal to get what we want. It robs us of our emotional maturity, stunting our growth at the age we began drinking and never allowing us to grow up because we drank our way through the lessons life had to teach us. Most importantly, alcoholism is a disease of a spiritual nature. I have found this to be the biggest component of all.

I believe that if I am bodily and mentally different from my fellows, which as an alcoholic I am, then I was born that way. And long before I took that very first drink, the signs were there. I always felt different, never a part of, always the black sheep of the family, the screw up, the one who would never amount to anything, and I was forever the chameleon. I had no idea who I was, just what other people told me I was. So I became the jock when I was with my soccer and softball friends, the bookworm when I was with my studious friends, and the partier when I was with my partying friends. But I was never me. And I never felt like I fit in anywhere, with any of these groups, which is probably why it was so easy to change in and out of personalities and appearances.

The one constant throughout my entire childhood, teenage years, young adulthood, and my entire adult life since, has been these feelings. A sense of this black hole within my gut that no matter how much booze, how much sex, how much partying, how many cigarettes, how many shopping trips, how much food, how much of anything and everything I could put inside of me, it would never ever fill up. This is the spiritual malady of our disease. I have since found relief from this black dismal abyss of nothingness and that is the presence of God in my life. And the only way I have ever known to get this relief is through the Program of Alcoholics Anonymous. It has filled the black hole in the pit of my stomach where nothing else has. And that is how I stay sober today. And sane.

When I first started attending A.A. meetings regularly, there was something that always kept me coming back. And that was the laughter in the rooms and the sparkle in people's eyes, the way their faces just lit up. I wanted that, desperately. I wanted to feel good, to feel joy and happiness. Then, I started hearing the word God getting thrown around more and more. Every time it came up, my heart would jump into my throat and race about. I wanted to swallow and run out of the room, but I couldn't move. More from embarrassment that everyone would be looking at me than anything else, but hey, if that's what kept me there, He knew how to get my attention. I didn't know what to think and I didn't know what to do, but I kept going back. I was not a religious person. At the time, I believed in God, I guess, but that was about it. I didn't attend church, hadn't since I was a child, and my only prayers were those "911" shout outs into the night sky, like, "just get me home safe and I promise I won't do it again."

The longer I stayed and listened and watched, the more I learned. And the less I feared. Then I realized that A.A. was not a religion, it did not preach or tell me how to act or be. And I learned that God could be whatever I wanted or needed Him to be—a Spirit, a Higher Power, a group of sober drunks or a meeting, heck, even a tree or a beach would do. Anything that was a power greater than myself. I learned it was just something there to help me, not hurt me, not rule over me, not judge or ridicule me, nor punish me. Nature worked for me for a long time, as did my Sponsors along the way. Because I have come to believe that I cannot get myself out of any mess with the same head that got me into it. I need outside help. And that is all the spiritual side of the Program is. Not playing God, not trying to be God, but feeling a part of the human race in a way I've never felt before. And that happens by doing God's work, which is simply helping others and getting out of self. Alcoholics are selfish, self-centered, self-seeking people full of self-delusion and self-pity. With this description, it is easy to see why an alcoholic's troubles are of his own making and that he is "an extreme example of self-will run riot." I love that line out of the Big Book. It's one of my favorites. Because it reminds me of all that I was and all that I could be again without A.A. and without my Higher Power.

Today, I have many freedoms. Most importantly, the freedom to live each day without the viscous cycle of drinking and stopping, and drinking and wanting to stop, and all of the chaos and insanity that went with it. But more than that are the underlying characteristic traits that come with being an alcoholic. This is truly a disease of perception and A.A. keeps me on the right path. This, in turn, allows me to live a full and rich life, not through material possessions, but through emotional and mental and physical freedoms and a continual process of growing and learning. I have found that Alcoholics Anonymous does for me, very, very slowly, what alcohol itself used to do for me very quickly. It gives me peace of mind and a joyful heart. It gives me relationships and friendships that are on a level I could have never experienced. It gives me mornings free from hangovers and regrets and remorse. It gives me the acceptance of love from others and the ability to love my fellow man. And it gives me a high better than any drink or drug ever could whenever I reach out my hand and help another human being, whether they are alcoholic or not.

I grew up in a family of six, but today, my family is much, much larger. I have many great friends who would do anything for me, any day, any time. And that is not something you can put in a bottle and buy.

I always thought I was a depressive person, always whining, sulking, complaining, or pissed off. But I have found by working this Program—participating in the Fellowship, going to meetings, taking on commitments, working the Twelve Steps, being of service, and helping others—that I am a rather optimistic and happy person who can now enjoy life like never before. Laughter does a lot to help the healing and I am grateful to the Program of Alcoholics Anonymous for showing me there is life, a good life, to be had after quitting drinking.

INTRODUCTION

The Need to Change

This manual has been written for a large group of people, all of whom have different personal problems and, of course, similar problems as well. As you read the workbook, you will find some ideas you have already learned, some ideas you are unable to accept, and some concepts that can really change your life. It would be nearly impossible to write an entire workbook just for one person. Therefore, read the workbook with an open mind, and seek the concepts you can accept to change your life. You may disagree with some concepts or feel the concept will not work for you. The concepts you don't think are good won't work for you. Tell the group or counselor why you feel something in particular will not work for you, and discuss the concept with your counselor. Maybe there is something more to it than you are seeing at this time. Be open about what you read and what you think.

If you are reading this manual, most likely you have been arrested for Driving Under the Influence (DUI). You may have not been drinking. It could have been another substance, which may be a legal substance (e.g. prescription medications), an illegal substance, or a combination of both. In either case, the treatment program and this workbook will work for you if you want it to. You probably have been through the Court process and are mandated to be in treatment. Many of you believe you do not need any treatment, and it's a matter of having better self-control? If this were truly the case, there would not be numerous individuals with multiple arrests. You may be one of them.

Before you came to your treatment facility, you thought about how to explain the situation for your arrest in a way that minimized the extent of your driving and drinking behaviors. If you didn't do this, I applaud you. Odds are you have been driving under the influence often, and the chances of getting arrested while you were drinking and driving just caught up with you. Don't worry, your therapist already knows this and has expected you to minimize the way you consume alcohol or other substances. Your therapist and group peers know you have been driving under the influence for quite some time. So be honest concerning your behaviors, and take accountability and responsibility in treatment. <u>Don't waste your time and money.</u>

FIRST STEP IN CHANGE

The first step in change is recognizing you have a problem. Often, a person may drink too much or abuse other substances, and his or her friends may often indicate that it's a problem. It is exactly like the person who drinks too much and his or her friends keep telling the person they have a serious problem. The person responds by saying or thinking, "these friends of mine are just wrong, I have things under control, I go to work everyday, I pay my bills on time, or I can control my substance use at anytime." These types of thoughts guarantee that you will never change. The moment you admit to yourself that you do have a problem with drinking, substance abuse, or anything destructive is the <u>FIRST STEP IN CHANGE</u>. If you continue to believe there is no problem, why change? This workbook can be used for a multitude of personal problems. The brain processes information in a very similar manner in all of us. We all have thoughts that create emotions, which drive our behaviors. <u>Controlling our thoughts and emotions is the key to interpersonal discipline and personal strength.</u> If we are unable to control our thoughts and emotions, then we are like a ship at sea with no captain. One or two things will surely happen. You will end up somewhere you don't want to be, or you will wreck. The more control we have of our thoughts and emotions, the more likely we will be successful in life. Conversely, individuals who have little control live in a world of chaos and drama as one bad situation happens after another. We all know people who live in drama and chaos, and it is primarily due to the inability to control thoughts, emotions and behaviors.

Changing your life can be very difficult, and it is for all people, whether we want to admit to it or not. We as humans become use to routine. We become accustomed to habits, as these actions makes life easy. The moment you step out of your comfort zone, feel like you need to change your behaviors, and recognize your past behaviors are self destructive, it will feel very uncomfortable, as in all new things we do with our lives. Discomfort, feeling a bit unsure, and recognizing our weaknesses are necessary steps to grow and live a productive life. Growth is often painful, and, therefore, many of us never change what needs to really change. All this sounds good, but is it worth all the stress and discomfort to be a better person and achieve all you want to be?

As the author of this manual, I personally don't believe in reincarnation, sorry. However, I do believe in Karma. I believe you have one life to live, and you don't get a second chance to make it right. Each day spent in the wrong direction is stepping backwards. Money will come and go, friends and parties will come and go, but you can never get back time. As you get much older, and trust me that day will come, you will look back on you life and either be happy or sad. If you look back on your life and never attempted to achieve your goals, did not accomplish much, or wasted your life in a perpetual state of intoxication, I guarantee you will be unhappy when you realize you can't go back and do things differently.

There was a research study conducted some years ago in which they asked several thousand retirees if they were happy with their lives. The one thing the study indicated was that the happiest individuals were those who attempted to "go for it." These individuals often achieved what they started, and even if they didn't, the fact that they had tried their best resulted in a happier life. On the other hand, the study indicated that the individuals who admitted to being sad or depressed were those who stayed inside their comfort zones, who never attempted to achieve their goals, and who never tried to explore new things or to change their lives. This is simply because they recognized when they were older that time is gone and that one chance to live a fulfilling life is gone forever. Think about that for a moment. You are no different. The time will come when you look back on how you spent your time in this life, and right now is the time to make better choices.

As a therapist, I have worked with many different individuals, and occasionally I run into the person who says his life has already been determined by God, Destiny if you will. I could not disagree with that more strongly. I believe God may know what we are going to do, but ultimately we make the choices with the direction and consequences of our actions. If you believe in destiny, then you have no control of your life. Here is a joke to prove my point.

One day a man is in his home by himself in a small town, and a truck pulls up with a couple of guys in the back telling him the dam is going to break, flood the town, and kill everyone that does not leave immediately. The man says to them, "if it's my destiny and God wants me to die, so be it." So, the men in the truck drive off. The dam breaks, and the man is now trapped on the second floor of his home as the water has flooded the first floor. A man in a boat comes by and says to the man stranded in the house, "jump on my boat before the water gets too high and you drown." The man says to him, "if it's my destiny and God wants me to die, so be it." Now the water gets even higher, and the man is now stranded on top of the roof. Suddenly there appears a helicopter, and the pilot yells to the man, "grab the rope, I will pull you up, it's your last chance or you will surely drown and die." The man says to the helicopter pilot, "if it's my destiny and God wants me to die, so be it." Well, the man drowns as could be expected. The man goes to heaven and meets God. The man says to God, "God why did you let me die." God replies, "You got to be kidding me. I sent you a truck, a boat, and I even sent a helicopter, what else did you want me to do for you?"

My belief, the joke illustrates well, that God more or less sits back and watches what we do and gives us all the tools we need to be successful. It's our choice to grab onto these opportunities or not. God, if you will, has provided to us all the things we need to be more healthy and happy, but it is still up to us to use them.

Start now by taking control of your life and making better and wiser decisions. Inaction leads to an unfulfilling and unhappy life, and chances are nothing of any real value will be accomplished. Take control of your life, find direction, make better choices, and be happy. <u>Happiness is a bi-product of good choices. Never, never forget that.</u> You are in treatment due to an accumulation of poor choices. This is your chance to turn your life around. Take advantage of this time, be invested in this material, and apply it to your everyday life.

The first step in change is to admit you have a problem with alcohol or other substances.

Honesty with your peers in groups, or in individual counseling sessions with your therapist, is your best bet to never get arrested for another DUI, living a much fuller life and to live a much fuller life. Not only do you have an opportunity to live a better life, you are paying for this service, and I might add—a lot of money for this treatment. Don't Waste It. Get the most benefit out of this time that you possibly can. The benefits you receive from treatment will last a lifetime. You will improve your relationships with your significant other, family members and co-workers. You will raise your self-esteem, focus on new goals in life, experience better health, and never be arrested again

GIVE IT YOUR BEST!!!

Phillip Karpinski, Licensed Clinical Therapist

CHAPTER 1

WHAT CAN I EXPECT IN TREATMENT?

Many people enter the treatment process with some idea of what to expect, while others have no clue about what to expect. In either case, you may have already thought of what personal information to divulge, what not to divulge about yourself, and perhaps a story as to why you were mandated for treatment, such as, circumstances which were primarily beyond your control or that it was a one time "thing." This line of thinking is much like taking your car to a mechanic after your car breaks down and giving the mechanic little or no information to help him fix your car. The final cost, as the mechanic goes through every system in the car, will always be higher, take much longer, and possibly never be fixed. Treatment is very much the same. You need to be honest with yourself and others.

This treatment manual uses the words Therapist, Psychologist, and Counselor interchangeably. Your group may be directed by either any of the three, and it largely depends on the professional degree the person has attained or how he or she would like to be addressed. If you are not sure of the proper way to address the group leader, just ask.

This treatment manual also uses "drinking" to mean the use of any substance that is destructive to your life. This could mean the use of marijuana, cocaine, over the counter medications, prescriptions, or whatever causes intoxication.

<u>If you really understood what the problems are in your life and how to correct these problems, you wouldn't be reading this manual.</u> This is not to say you are incompetent, but realize there are times when we don't recognize our lives have taken a wrong turn, and outside feedback and professional help is needed. Your therapist knows there are numerous other things you could be doing with your time. Some of you will come to treatment taking a "Victim Stance." This means you want others to feel sorry for all the hardships your arrest has created for you, and that you believe you are now the victim. Many people spend too much time complaining about how unfair all of this has been. For example, if it wasn't for that "unscrupulous Judge" having a bad day, mandating you to complete treatment, pay fines, or do community service, the last place you would be is in treatment. Does that sound about right? For those of you who now fully understanding that alcohol has been a destructive force in your life, treatment will be exciting and a learning experience with benefits which will last the rest of your life. If you feel this is going to be a positive and rewarding experience, then you are on the right path. Don't worry if others

are not on the same page as you—the rest of your group members will catch up. Just give them time to recognize the benefits.

The treatment process is very much like attending a college course on Psychology. Treatment addresses how we think, how we react to our environment, how we view ourselves in the world, and how to make better decisions to be more productive and successful in life. Of course, the main point of treatment is never to take any substance while operating a vehicle, but if we don't change our thoughts and the associated reasons for drinking, then nothing will change, and the chances of being arrested or harming someone else again continues.

Research indicates that group treatment (i.e. involvement with peers with similar problems) may be as productive as individual counseling. It has been proven that group treatment is highly effective. The reasoning behind this is complex. Often we can see ourselves in others. Their inappropriate behaviors seem to stand out, and the "ah hah" experience happens. You say to yourself, "that is exactly what I do, and I am experiencing the same problems." The other effective part of group therapy is being confronted by your peers. Peers recognize when you are being dishonest, denying issues in your life as a problem, or minimizing inappropriate behaviors and the impact of these behaviors on you, your family, friends and the community as a whole. Therapists are thrilled to watch a group member point out another member's denial, minimization, or justification of a poor behavior. Suggestions and feedback are very powerful when it comes from a peer in treatment, more so than when a therapist points it out. Group members often feel the therapist is paid to say certain things, because he or she works for the state or the local municipality. When a group member states an opinion, however, it comes from the heart and needed to be said. There are times when a group leader may use confrontation with you, and maybe it's you arguing too much, or thinking "What a waste of time. I don't need this group," or generally exhibiting a poor attitude. Appropriate confrontation is a good thing. Appropriate confrontation helps in several ways. Appropriate confrontation is a way to let you know your thinking is not on target without being offensive to you. It gives you the opportunity to think about how you view your thoughts and actions in a different light. It can sometimes be more powerful when a group peer gives feedback. A professional is trained to recognize thinking distortions, but when a peer gives feedback this means the problem is more obvious, even to the average person, and the feedback needs to be taken seriously. This is another person in your situation trying to help you.

Most individuals come to group with a fear of exposing personal weakness to others in the group. A personal weakness, or flaw if you will, is exactly why you are in group, which is to make change and be a better person. If you cannot overcome the fear of discussing a personal issue in groups, let your therapist know this and set up an individual counseling session for more privacy. Your therapist will work with you and guide you with a level of confidentiality. Not speaking of a particular problem is unacceptable. You will be doomed to repeat the same poor behavior, and the problem will never be resolved. If you are reading this treatment manual in group, then your therapist has certain expectations of you while you attend the group. Honest participation is imperative. In other words, just completing the homework assignments and attending each group on time may not be enough. If you are not open and honest with the group, you may not be discharged successfully. Ask the counselor of his or her expectations of participation in the treatment program, and how participate at a higher level.

Treatment is based on trust with your therapist and group members. If a person does not trust his or her therapist, then it is unlikely the person will follow the therapist's suggestions. Many people have never been to a group meeting, and they may fear saying something embarrassing or looking less smart than others. You need to have faith that your counselor is there to help and never make anyone appear to be stupid or less than other members of the group. You can bet the other group members are experiencing similar feelings. As you become familiar with your peers, a level of trust will certainly grow.

Another component making the group process effective is to "Problem Solve." This means each member gives a verbal report in the beginning of group to their peers, and this is often referred to as "Issues." Groups usually start off with personal issues (i.e. problems) for two reasons. First, it gives the group member time to vent his/her frustrations to the other group members that might be experiencing similar problems, or at least individuals who are ready to sympathize and empathize. The anxiety caused by many personal problems can be alleviated just by telling someone you trust. Secondly, the group helps build better problem solving skills. This takes place as you give and hear suggestions by other group members about what they would do with a particular problem.

The venting of problems in groups helps to relieve stress. Research has suggested one of the reasons why women live longer than men may be due to releasing negative emotions on a more continuous basis, which can be expressed by crying or venting frustrations to friends or family. When you are in treatment, it may be difficult at first to really talk about how you are feeling or how past experiences have affected you. Once you learn to vent your frustrations positively, to express your emotions, you will notice a level of closeness with friends and family you had never thought possible. Maybe this is one of the reasons you are reading this manual. Maybe you have a history of bad relationships and have become sad and lonely and drink to give you a feeling of relief. Eventually, you will learn that all of your life experiences linked together and created <u>the person sitting in the chair reading this right now</u> . . . . And the person sitting and reading this right now is YOU. You need some sort of help, or you wouldn't be here. All of your life experiences, good and bad decisions, created the person reading this workbook at this time.

If you start to say to yourself that this DUI was a one-time thing, and <u>"I won't ever do this again," I would have to bet you will DO IT AGAIN.</u> You will need to address what thoughts and behaviors led you to read this workbook and change those things, and then you have an excellent chance of never being arrested again. In fact, if you follow this manual completely, you will never be arrested again. Think about that one for a while!!!

There is one main point of the treatment process everyone must keep in mind at all times during the course of your program. Anyone can learn the materials presented in treatment. It's not that hard. It is the people who use, integrate and apply what they have learned in treatment into their everyday lives who become successful. If you don't use and put into action what you have learned—nothing will be gained—nothing will change, and you will continue to move sideways in your life until you finally crash and burn. You may also maybe bring someone else down with you. Don't waste your time and money and think you know "it" already, because you don't. You wouldn't have been arrested or mandated for treatment. Consider yourself lucky you were arrested. That can be hard to believe, but it's true. Think for a moment if in the future you killed someone in a car accident, maybe your family is joyous that you are finally getting help, or the next time you are arrested you spend time in jail and lose your friends, job, and family.

Have you ever heard the saying, "For every cloud, there is a Silver Lining?" I believe this is absolutely true. In essence, life seems to repeat itself in very specific patterns. Go figure, but it does; and for every bad thing that happens to you, something good comes out of it. Your arrest may help you save yourself from jail or from injuring yourself and possibly others.

The benefits of treatment last a life time. Don't kid yourself; this is going to take discipline and effort to change your life. Feel good in knowing many people do change their lives every day. A helpful hint in treatment is to walk out the door of your treatment facility and place one new thing you learned into practice everyday. Pick one thing every day you learn in treatment that you feel will help change your life, and apply it to your life. Use it, Use it, Use it, Use it . . . Repeat it until it becomes a habit. Do not attempt to make several important changes all at once. This may become overwhelming, and a sense of failure or a sense of being overwhelmed; or a sense that change is impossible may overcome you. <u>Make a list of the most important things you learned and write them down. Keep the list where you can see it every day until the things you learned become habits. Put this list on the door of your bedroom or tape it to a refrigerator where you see it every day.</u> You will learn many treatment concepts to help, but everyone is different. The great thing about this is you get to pick and choose what will work for you. Don't think nothing will work for you. That's just wrong thinking. <u>Remember, "IF YOU THINK YOU CAN—OR YOU THINK YOU CAN'T—YOU ARE RIGHT."</u>

There are those who will experience certain defense mechanisms, which must be overcome. A **Defense Mechanism**, and we all have them, is basically protecting our pride by blaming events or others for our mistakes. Think for a minute. I would bet you have used a defense mechanism this week. Did someone say something to you that led you to put the blame on another person or thing or to claim that the situation was out of your control? Did you convince yourself that a task was done incorrectly because someone or something else was at fault?

Some believe their therapists are working for the "man" and fear disclosing their past or present poor/bad behaviors. Speak to the therapist about your drinking behaviors. Get a full understanding of the consequences if you admit in group or to your therapist that you are currently drinking while in treatment. Your treatment contract will most likely have a no-drinking clause. What are the possible consequences if you break it? Will I get kicked out of treatment and have to go in front of a judge again? Do I get another chance? What happens next? Be clear with your therapist if you have a problem with drinking or other substances. This won't be easy. Tell your therapist that you have a problem, and you are on the road to being successful. All treatment providers desire and thank clients for this honesty. Make an agreement with your therapist about drinking while in treatment. I am sure all therapists will respect that honesty. Some therapists may not give you that chance, so find out exactly the rules of the treatment agreement you signed. If you have not signed a treatment contract, you should have. Ask for it. The rules governing the consequences of a **Relapse** (i.e. alcohol or substance use during the course of treatment) is up to your treatment provider and the court.

Generally, you can expect to be randomly drug tested. There are tests now, which are able to give an accurate account of your substance behaviors over a week period. Being dishonest in treatment is the worst thing to do. If you are caught lying about one thing, your therapist will think you may be lying about other things as well. On the other hand, being honest with your therapist lets him/her know you are serious about getting help, and he/she will go over the top to help you. Don't use your therapist's good will as a way to do what you want, and definitely do not expect to come to treatment and explain the wonderful weekend you had at the local pub. I am pretty sure you will be kicked out of treatment and meet that unscrupulous judge again.

For many of you, the hardest part of treatment is getting over the idea of not having alcohol in your life anymore. For most of you, complete abstinence from alcohol is the only answer. This has been the hardest part for almost everyone to accept and abide. Each holiday, each weekend, and, for some of you every night, alcohol has been a habitual part of your plans. It's hard to imagine going out with your friends and not drinking. How is it possible to be at social events when I am nervous and not drink to loosen up? It's even harder to think about never drinking again. Alcohol has been a part of your life for so long, and so often it may feel like the focus of your life is to finish work then drink, which brings up the questions, "what will I do with myself? How will I fill all my time? How can I handle boredom? How am I going to deal with all the STRESS? Won't my friends think I am boring?" Treatment will address all of these very common concerns. All successful members from AA will tell you how life is so much better without drinking. For example, no more hangovers, no more being late on bills, no more losing jobs, no more losing relationships, and no more ridiculous arguments.

During your sobriety, you will experience that friends of yours and acquaintances will treat you differently. This happens to everyone in the beginning stages of sobriety. When you go to places where your friends are consuming alcohol and you decline to drink, expect a reaction, and this reaction is usually negative. You may expect to hear, "What's wrong with you? Come on, one drink won't hurt. Don't be a bore." Or, maybe your friends will pull away from you. The reason for this is that these people feel a bit ashamed as they perceive you having better self-control, sense of purpose, and discipline. People that drink far too often know they have little self-control, and you declining a drink makes them feel uncomfortable to the point they may avoid you. Sorry if your friends react that way, and if they do—then you have to question if they really were a friend or just a party buddy. A good friend will applaud you and be happy for you. Don't worry about those who don't applaud your effort. Yes, it will feel a bit lonely at first, but eventually you will weed out the destructive people in your life.

Now here is the good part of successful treatment. How will it feel when you meet people and they admire the way you look, meaning very healthy? How will it feel when you wake up every morning feeling like a million dollars and don't have to nurse yourself back to health each morning by overeating, lying in bed all day, or drinking excessive coffee, attempting to hide your hangover at work and get some energy back? How will it feel when you buy a vacation home next to a beach or near a lake in the mountains? These things are all very possible. You just forgot, or didn't believe you could get them, or thought you didn't deserve them. You would be right to think you didn't deserve the better things in life if you spent all your time drinking. **In fact, people who get drunk all the time are losers. This is not meant to be mean or hurtful, but it needs to be said.**

The big question for those of you who drink all the time and do not believe you can succeed is where did you get the idea you were a loser? Possibly, somewhere, somehow, somebody put the idea in your head that you would not amount to anything. Maybe you lack confidence to succeed in life because you miserably failed at several ideas, relationships, or business ventures. Maybe you had poor grades in school and were made fun of at school for "being stupid." Let me tell you this as a fact. Making mistakes is part of life and a good thing. Failing at something is just letting you know you need to change the way you are doing something, and there is a better way to do it. It's that simple. A great example of this is Tom Monaghan. He started Domino's Pizza. This man is a hero for all of us. At his first attempt to start a pizza delivery service he went bankrupt. On the second attempt to start a pizza delivery service he went bankrupt again. My God, who has the courage to go bankrupt on two occasions and attempts to do it again? Well he did. He gave a third try to make the pizza delivery service work. He is now worth millions, and I believe he owns his own baseball team. There are several points to be made here. Each time he failed he did not give up, and neither should you. Each time he failed there was a lesson he learned about how to do a better job the next time. He became successful, and so can you.

Your treatment provider recognizes that if you are happy, successful, gain a higher level of self-esteem, learn better communication skills, handle stress better, are better able to solve problems, and reach a higher level of self-control, the chances of you abusing any substance is minimal. The opposite is just as true. If you lack these essential human qualities, you are surely going to self medicate on something, whether it is alcohol, drugs, gambling or overeating. You will look for something to hide from your problems.

Treatment will make you feel better about yourself and help you resolve your problems much more easily. This is fantastic, but don't forget the main point: never drive intoxicated again. This is the ultimate goal of your treatment. This brings me to a story of a woman I had as a client who was going to AA meetings and seeking counseling services. This person was getting "high" before the AA meetings, whether it was a shot of liquor or hit off the pot pipe. She began telling me of the benefits from AA meetings and how much it made her feel better. I explained to her that she was missing the point. This went on for 20 minutes as "I truly did not understand" what she was trying to tell me. I replied, "has it changed the way you drink or take other substances?" "But that's not what I am talking about," she replied, "You don't understand. I feel better about myself and feel less stressed." Again, I replied, "has it changed the way you take alcohol or substances?" Finally, she recognized the meetings are for just that point. Stop drinking and getting high. Period.

Treatment and AA meetings are for just that: Abstinence. This last story will apply to many others as they will feel better about themselves while in AA. They see hope and feel better about themselves but rationalize one way or the other to continue the same behaviors. Many will say, "I will only drink at home. This will keep me safe." After 4 or 5 drinks, anyone can rationalize why they can drive to a friend's house or to the corner store for a couple of more beers, wine or cigarettes, which is only 2 blocks away. It's not a problem. I won't get caught. Wrong thinking and bad choices go hand-in-hand, and eventually something will go drastically wrong in your life. Who really wants that???

Complete the following Exercises.

List 5 things you learned reading this chapter?

_____
_____
_____
_____
_____
_____
_____
_____
_____
_____
_____
_____

What were the most important ideas you learned, and why are they important to you?

_____
_____
_____
_____
_____
_____
_____
_____
_____
_____
_____
_____
_____
_____

Chapter 2

Main Components of Treatment

TALK ABOUT EVENTS IN YOUR LIFE

During treatment, you can expect to talk about your entire life. The question is why? As you are reading this, at this very moment, you are a compilation of every thought and event in your life, which makes you—You. All of your life experiences and choices have led you to be reading this manual at this moment. This didn't happen by accident.

Recent research suggests the majority of the personality is formed in the first four years of life. Researchers believe a child of this age views the world as scary and unpredictable. When a baby cries and the parents do not respond to the baby by picking the child up and/or feeding the baby, it is likely the child will grow up as an insecure person. We have all witnessed adults that constantly seek attention, approval, and jump into one relationship after a breakup, only to find themselves in another immediate relationship. It is extremely hard to be in a relationship when you continually have to re-enforce a needy person's fear of rejection or disapproval. Possibly during your teen years, and we all know how mean kids can be in school, you were picked on and made fun of, and that has changed your personality. Instead of being an assertive person, standing up for yourself, and meeting your needs and wants, things just go by and nothing is done to grasp an opportunity. Your present behavior is a result of all your experiences. All of us have some event that has changed the way we perceive our place in the world and how we interact with others. A severe breakup in a relationship can change the way we view the opposite sex and can create fear in forming another relationship. Financial hardships change the way we spend money. All past events in your life shape how you view the world and how you react to each and every situation. You are most likely unaware of this fact. Your reactions to situations are based on previous events. This is what therapy is about: recognizing that our past experiences shape our current reactions and how to react to events differently or change the way we perceive events. This happens in therapy by making a more confident person, raising self-esteem, being assertive, resolving personal conflict, and outlining a plan for life to be more successful.

If being successful and happy is something you want and desire, treatment is the place for you, and I believe everyone can benefit from self-examination. I don't know one person who doesn't think he or she can make his or her life better. This is why people spend $20,000 dollars for a week with Tony Robins. These folks that can afford $20,000 are already financially successful and are looking to gain more out of life. You too can gain more out of life and become financially successful. Your treatment provider will want you to look at all aspects of your life and help you identify areas or issues causing problems and/or improve on the accomplishments in place. Remember, money comes and goes, but you never get back time. Don't waste this precious time on living in a fog. You really want to take advantage of this time. Write down some of the problems in your life now; get ready to jump in groups or individual counseling and discuss your life. If you are not quite sure what you need to change, your therapist will help you. But don't use this as an excuse to not write the list of 5 things in the next exercise section, because none of them are wrong.

Before we get to the main points of treatment, you will need to understand the term **Compartmentalizing.** This is where you believe each problem is separate and not related to other problems in your life. Compartmentalizing is a failure to understand that there is a direct relationship between your different problems. For example, if you are drinking too much and having problems at work, or with your relationship, and believe there is no connection between them, you are "Compartmentalizing." Your problems are interconnected. It would be hard to image someone drinking all the time and it not affecting your relationship, work, or health.

THE MAIN PARTS OF TREATMENT

BE HONEST IN TREATMENT

First, you have to recognize and admit a problem(s) exists, and treatment is all about you. If you believe you don't have any problems, this guarantees you won't change. Only when a person admits a problem exists will there by any change. Recognize you are spending your money for treatment, and get the most of it by admitting to behaviors in your life that have been problematic. Be honest in treatment. Your therapist already knows there are issues and problems in your life that need to be addressed, and there is nothing you will tell your therapist he/she has not already heard from someone else. You may have different twists and turns in your life compared to others, but potholes and bumps in the road are similar. Your therapist is qualified to help you. Be non-judgmental, and keep your information confidential within the scope of the law. Your therapist will often be confrontational (i.e. in your face) to your behaviors in an appropriate manner. Appropriate confrontation is a very good thing, as you will need a push to make significant changes in your life. You don't have to worry about being put down or feeling any less human in treatment, because everyone else in the group has similar problems. You can bet your therapist has hit a few potholes in his or her life as well. You may consider asking questions about your therapist's life, but the object of treatment is for you, not for your therapist to talk about his or her personal life. Often therapists do give personal stories of problems they have encountered, and this can be done to bring home a particular point or help you understand how they overcame a particular problem. Just remember that you are there for you, your family, and friends.

Denial or Minimizing

The most common problem treatment providers have to overcome with clients is **Minimizing** or **Denying** by the client a problem exists. Minimizing means making a problem or inappropriate event smaller than it is really. Minimizing can come in many different forms. For example, telling your therapist it was "one time thing to drink and drive," or "I have never drank that much before in my life," or "I can't believe my blood alcohol was at that level. I only had 3 drinks all night." The reason behind minimizing is to protect our Ego. Everyone has a defense response when we feel our self worth is being attacked. If you closely examine your week, there is a very good chance you have done this several times. You are no different than anyone else. We all attempt to protect our Egos. Yes, pride, or Ego if you will, is going to get in the way of your treatment being successful. Very few people are totally honest in treatment, especially in the beginning of treatment. This is going to be a major hurdle to overcome, as no one wants to admit he or she is less than competent or doesn't have control of his or her life. **Denial** means nothing happened at all. This very rarely happens in treatment, as it is hard to deny a blood test as being accurate, but therapists have seen this behavior on occasion. Some clients will deny the accuracy of a breathalyzer, but that is really minimizing the problem.

There are several different types of denial.

a) Denial of Intent. This is when people state they had no intention of getting drunk and driving; it just happened.

b) Denial of Responsibility. This is when people state the circumstances made them drive under the influence.

c) Denial of the Facts. The blood test was inaccurate. I know I was not that intoxicated.

DEVELOP A TREATMENT PLAN (YOUR GOALS DURING TREATMENT)

While you are in treatment, a "Treatment Plan" will be developed with the help of your therapist. This is a concise guide or direct course of action to help change your life. Take it seriously, and be honest with the therapist. A treatment plan is what is expected of you to change in your life and an agreement with your therapist of what his/her role is during the treatment process. The first part of the Treatment Plan or Treatment Contract will obviously state "no consumption of any substance" during the course of treatment without the written permission from a medical doctor.

YOUR BEHAVIORS HAVE BEEN DESTRUCTIVE TO YOUR LIFE

After admitting to behaviors in your life that have been less than admirable, you need to understand fully how these behaviors have been a destructive force in your life and in the lives of others. This includes your family, friends, co-workers, and members of the community. Most likely you have put all these people at risk, caused them to worry, or have strained your relationships in the past, and possibly this is an on going problem now. Let's be honest. How many people want to be around someone intoxicated? The conversation seems child-like and the behavior matches. How many couples have you known that break up due to someone drinking too often or making fools of themselves and embarrassing the other person. Therapists usually expect to see substance abuse from one or both partners when it comes to marriage and family counseling. Substance abuse will eventually destroy a relationship or a marriage. Ask anyone, and 9 out of 10 times you will hear drugs or alcohol was the issue, or something to the effect there was constant arguing when drugs or alcohol was involved.

Your treatment provider will help you evaluate the important areas of your life and help you see how the use of alcohol or substances has been destructive to your well-being.

THE OFFENSE CYCLE (HOW & WHY DID THIS HAPPEN TO ME)

During the treatment process you will be expected to write out an "offense cycle." This is a description of events before and surrounding your arrest and the history of your behaviors and thoughts. This is an extremely important aspect of treatment. The offense cycle is all of the thoughts, habits, emotions, thinking distortions, and previous behaviors leading to an arrest. You may not be aware there was a pattern to your behavior that is predicable and reproducible. Each time you have a drinking episode, there is usually a predictable pattern of events. There is a chapter in this manual devoted to the Offense Cycle, and you will be expected to write it out and present this to your therapist and/or group peers.

The offense cycle is necessary to complete as you can then understand what caused your behavior. The only way you can prevent something negative from happening again is by understanding what caused it in the first place. After you leave the treatment program, possibly years later, if you recognize similar problems in your life are occurring again, there is a much better chance you can use the material you learned to prevent the same situation from happening again.

A more descriptive list of these patterns is in the Offense Cycle Chapter.

THE RELAPSE PREVENTION PLAN

Relapse means drinking and driving again. Relapse does not mean getting arrested again, though you just got lucky for not being arrested. The Relapse Prevention Plan is your written plan presented to your peers and therapists in group or individual counseling on how you are going to keep you and the community safe. When you present your relapse plan to your group peers, your words impact others and your presentation helps you retain and maintain the treatment tools learned. There are two very important words in your treatment program: **Avoid** and **Escape**. Part of your relapse plan will discuss how you will avoid high-risk situations (e.g. places where you consume alcohol), and how to escape a high risk situation appropriately.

Questions

1) List at least 5 things you want to change in your life.

   a) _____
   _____

   b) _____
   _____

   c) _____
   _____

   d) _____
   _____

   e) _____
   _____

2) List 4 reasons you need to be honest in treatment.

   a) _____

   b) _____

   c) _____

   d) _____

3) List 5 benefits can you expect from abstinence from alcohol.

   a) _____

   b) _____

   c) _____

   d) _____

   e) _____

4) How is abstinence from alcohol going to make your life more difficult?

   _____
   _____

_____

_____

5)   What problems has alcohol brought into your life? (Don't list your arrest)

_____
_____
_____
_____
_____
_____
_____

6)   What is a Defense Mechanism?

_____
_____
_____
_____
_____
_____

7)   Why would someone use a defense mechanism in treatment?

_____
_____
_____
_____
_____

8   How honest are you going to be in treatment? (0-100%) _____
_____

Chapter 3

Understanding the Abuse of Alcohol

This chapter will discuss the damaging effects of alcohol. That is the mental and physical problems for those that abuse alcohol. Alcohol does not just affect the person consuming. There are secondary victims throughout due to the abuse of alcohol. A secondary victim of alcohol use or abuse could be the mother of a child run over by a drunk driver, a wife who puts up with an abusive husband every day, or the children in the home who hear the constant yelling and screaming.

Approximately 38 people die each day across our country by the drunk driver. If you were wondering what the legal limit to drive under the influence is, there is none. Each state will use a baseline, such as .08%, but the reality is that if you fail a field sobriety test you can still be charged with operating a vehicle under the influence.

Research points to the following facts: approximately 84% of all murders are by individuals who are intoxicated on alcohol; and the majority of our prisons are populated by individuals who were consuming alcohol or some other illegal substance and unable to control their behaviors. Alcohol is considered a dis-inhibitor, which means that we often make very poor choices while intoxicated and do behaviors we would never do under normal circumstances. The ability to make a rational decision goes right out the window, and one moment in our lives can change our entire future.

Many of us consider the most dangerous individuals in society are sex offenders, drug dealers, gang members or some other unsavory characters. Have you ever thought the most dangerous person in your life could be the person living in your home? Domestic violence has become rampant, and most of the deaths associated with domestic violence are due to intoxication on alcohol and a tumultuous relationship. If you abuse alcohol, you could very well be the person who is at most risk to hurt your family. Most people never consider themselves to be the person that should be feared.

HISTORY OF ALCOHOL

Throughout history, human beings have consumed alcohol for various purposes. Many cultures started using it as a religious beverage or a drink that was necessary to sustain life. Ancient China and Egypt consumed it during spiritual rituals. Early Egypt also drank alcoholic beverages because it was believed that they were essential substances for an individual's existence. Though there are alcoholic beverages that have some health benefits, such as moderate wine consumption reducing cardiovascular and heart disease, alcoholic use/abuse has dire consequences on the health of an individual. Abuse of alcohol leads to intoxication, pancreas and liver damage, as well as children born with alcohol fetal syndrome. Mentally, people have experienced short-term effects such as blackouts, or they develop long-term damage such as **Wernicke-Korsakoff Syndrome**. Studies have shown that abuse and prolonged use is devastating on the human body.

There are many well-documented studies which demonstrate the different adverse affects alcohol has physically on the human body. According to Dr. Michaele P. Dunlap, whose article "Biological Impacts of Alcohol Use: An Overview" studied the harmful effects of alcohol on the body: "Alcohol is not digested like other foods. Instead of being converted and transported to cells and tissues, it avoids the normal digestive process and goes directly to the blood stream." The article further demonstrates that " . . . only 20 percent of alcohol is absorbed directly into the blood through the stomach walls and 80 percent is absorbed into the bloodstream through the small intestine." Because of the high, distinctive resemblance between alcohol and water, alcohol adulterates itself in the water volume of the body, such as the tissues, in order to travel through the system. Alcohol then permeates the liver, brain, kidneys, and every other major organ and tissue system in the body within minutes after ingestion. This means the concentration level of alcohol is extremely high when entering each organ and tissue system in the body because proper digestion has not taken place. The rate of absorption depends on how diluted the alcohol is, which means the more pure alcoholic beverages are, the faster the speed of amalgamation into the organs and tissues. If alcohol is ingested in high or concerted amounts, it can be devastating initially and have long-term adverse affects on the stomach and small intestine. Alcohol taken in concentrated amounts can irritate the stomach lining to the extent that it produces a sticky mucous which delays absorption. The pylorus valve, which connects the stomach and small intestine, may go into a spasm in the presence of concentrated alcohol, trapping the alcohol in the stomach instead of passing it on to the small intestine where it would be more rapidly absorbed into the blood stream. The stomach lining may become inflamed and irritated, which may lead to vomiting. The temperature of the alcoholic beverage has an effect on the rate of absorption, meaning the warmer the drink, the faster the amalgamation. If an individual continuously drinks alcohol on a regular basis, the damage to the stomach will be severe. In the book "Psychology: Themes and Variations," Dr. Wayne Weiten states that long-term use of alcohol will cause "gastritis and ulcers." The stomach and small intestines are not the only organs affected by alcohol consumption. Goodenough, et al., 2007, explained how harmful this substance is on the liver. "Excessive alcohol consumption damages the liver, an organ that performs many vital functions in the body." They further state, "Alcohol metabolism preempts fat metabolism in the liver, causing fats to accumulate in liver cells. Four or five drinks daily for several weeks are enough to cause fat accumulation to begin." If people quit this habit early on, liver cells are not yet damaged, and if they practice abstinence, their livers can be completely healed. But, continuous drinking will cause the buildup of fat. This will cause the liver cells to expand, even to the point where it will either rupture or develop cysts that substitute in place of the regular cells. Other liver problems resulting from prolonged alcoholic abuse include **Alcoholic Hepatitis** caused from inflammation, and **Cirrhosis**, which is fibrous scar tissue.

Short-term psychological impairments are often disregarded as side effects, which is a dangerous misconception. Alcohol abuse or use can affect the mentality of an individual both short-term and long-term because the brain is the first organ in the body that is affected by the substance. According to Dr. Michaele P. Dunlap, "The brain is the organ that is most affected by alcohol, and proves that it is being damaged through the drinker's behavior changes and emotional distress. Three noticeable effects of alcohol injury to the brain include memory loss, confusion, and augmentation (a physiological response to alcohol which results in hyper-alertness to normal situations.)" (Dunlap, 2010). Examples include extreme change in a person's behavior or mood, or becoming extremely sensitive to light and sound. A person drinking alcohol also may experience blackouts or memory loss. That is why there have been individuals who report waking up the day after heavily drinking and not remembering the events that happened on the prior night. This happens because alcohol reduces the amount of oxygen to the brain, which kills thousands of brain cells while an individual is intoxicated. Because the brain is a vital part of the central nervous system, the entire body is affected once the brain is impaired through alcohol use. "Although it weighs only about three pounds and could be held in one hand, the brain contains billions of interacting cells that integrate information from inside and outside the body, coordinate the body's actions, and enable us to talk, think, remember, plan, create, and dream" (Weiten, 2008). Because sensory impulses are sent out to the central nervous system and motor signals distribute from it, the entire body becomes impaired. Intoxication is the result, which means normal bodily functions such as pain sensors, taste, and smell are all altered. Because alcohol is a depressant, emotional and sensory functions are affected and judgment, memory and learning abilities are all disturbed. As a result, individuals who have been drinking may act out by behaving out of character due to a loss of inhibition. According to research performed at the Harvard School of Public Health (Wechsler et al., 2002), it was found that once alcohol consumption freed an individual's inhibitions, there were drinkers who were prone to argue or act aggressively. In a survey conducted by this group, 29% of the students who did not engage in binge drinking reported they had been victims of insults or humiliation by drunken individuals. Further statistics within the study revealed 19% had been involved in a serious argument, 9% had been physically assaulted, and 19.5% had been subjected to unwanted sexual advances (Wechsler et al., 2002). According to Weiten, 2008, " . . . alcohol appears to contribute to about 90% of student rapes and 95% of violent crime on campus. Such disastrous short-term consequences resulting from alcohol abuse can ruin or destroy the lives of the drinker and those around them. Long-term effects can be equally, if not more, catastrophic."

Continued alcohol abuse over a long period of time may cause irreparable damage to the central nervous system. Long-term effects of alcohol on the central nervous system include tolerance, dependency, and irreversible damage. Developing a high tolerance, as well as an increase in dependency, is the result of the changes taking place in the brain due to the length of alcoholic intake. Tolerance can develop after a period of chronic alcohol exposure (protracted tolerance) or after a single dose (acute tolerance). Since the brain cells do not restore themselves, important parts of the brain such as the reward pathway become permanently damaged due to tolerance and dependency on alcohol. Alcohol also suppresses the excitatory nerve cells and augments the effects of the inhibitory neurotransmitter GABA. By enhancing an inhibitor, an individual will experience a sluggish effect. Once the brain becomes dependant on alcohol, the addict will need the depressant in order to function throughout the day. Another serious problem resulting from prolonged alcohol abuse is an individual developing Wernicke-Korsakoff Syndrome. According to the National Institute on Alcohol Abuse and Alcoholism website, they found that, "Up to 80 percent of alcoholics, however, have a deficiency in Thiamine, and some of these people will go on to develop serious brain disorders such as Wernicke-Korsakoff syndrome." Wernicke-Korsakoff syndrome is an illness that contains two conditions. As defined by Weiten, 2002, Wernicke syndrome is, "an acute condition characterized by mental confusion and ocular abnormalities," while Korsakoff syndrome is, " . . . a psychotic condition characterized by impairment of memory and learning, apathy, and degeneration of the white brain matter" (Weiten, 2002) Each person who has Wernicke syndrome does not necessarily develop Korsakoff syndrome, as 10-20% never develop the latter. The symptoms of Wernicke's are severe. For example, patients who have developed this syndrome have difficulties entering and exiting rooms and may even forget how to walk. Although every impairment may not show in an individual who has abused alcohol for years, each addict will develop some psychological problems as a result of misusing.

Alcohol/Substances and Pregnancy

Women abusing, or even drinking alcohol recreationally while pregnant, will affect the fetal development of their unborn child. This is known as Fetal Alcohol Syndrome (FAS) and may cause the child to have mental retardation, growth deficiencies, and characteristic facial features (i.e. facial features that are abnormal). Experienced therapists have witnessed children with FAS and report that all of them suffer from similar cognitive and behavioral problems. Children that have been exposed during pregnancy have these common factors: <u>Learning Disorders, ADHD (Hyperactivity), Anger/Aggression, and Impulsivity.</u> Taking substances during pregnancy is dangerous to the development of the unborn child's brain, especially during the first trimester. The damage to the unborn child is life long. Without going into complex neurology, areas of the unborn child's brain are not developed correctly, and the child will experience cognitive, emotional, and behavioral problems. The child will usually experience an inability to read well or understand and comprehend what was read. The child will experience lifelong problems in school, such as continual poor grades, meaning the child usually has to be placed in an Individual Educational Program. Children who are exposed to substance use, not just abuse, generally are hyperactive and unable to focus on the easiest of tasks. This is not only at school, but is in the home as well. The inability to focus for any length of time on anything makes it impossible for the child to stay on task, such as doing any chores in the home, without being told many times before the task is completed. Children who are exposed exhibit anger and aggression at school and in the home throughout their lives and often have problems as adults as well. Several parts of the brain work in conjunction to control emotional situations (e.g. Frontal Cortex, Parietal Lobe, Temporal Lobe, and the Amygdale). For example, the child is confronted by a negative emotional situation in which the nervous system becomes overactive. The child is unable to use the Frontal Cortex, the part of the brain that problem solves and helps one make appropriate choices, and the child acts out with whatever thought comes first, which is often a level of aggression or anger. As we all know, our first choices in problem situations are not usually the best, as anger and frustration takes over, and children with neurological problems do poorly.

This makes for a chaotic life in the home as parents struggle on a daily basis with the child. Parents often come to therapy and complain that their child can't follow through on any direction they give the child, or the child continually gets frustrated or angry. <u>The answer for the parents is that since the mother was drinking or taking substances during pregnancy, the child can do</u>

no different. Parents have a difficult time understanding the child just can't be better. Of course the parents want some medication to help, and the child is put on some medication for most of its teen years and sometimes at an earlier age. This affects the child's self-esteem, as he or she is aware other children in school are smarter and have more self-control. The child is aware certain occupations will always be outside of his or her reach, such as a doctor, or any other profession that entails a high level of education or college degree of substance.

We end up with a child who feels less than others in school (i.e. experiences Low Self Esteem), who has anger/aggression as a general part of his or her history, who experiences a high level of hyperactivity on a daily basis, and who has behaviors that are hard to control (i.e. impulsivity). When we put this altogether one can only imagine what the child's life will be like. The child while attending school will not considered smart by his or her peers, will associate with other children who use aggression as a way to deal with emotional problems, and who will be well aware other peers in school have a far better chance to succeed in life. The child will most likely associate with other children that are similar, and from here one can only imagine where some of the criminal classes of society are first developed.

Delirium Tremens

Prolonged heavy drinking causes delirium tremens. The majority of people who develop this had a history of drinking around 4-5 pints of wine or 7-8 pints of beer or hard alcohol every day for several months. Also, those who had a 10-year history of habitual alcohol use, otherwise known as "alcoholism," usually develop delirium tremens. Symptoms usually occur within 72 hours after the last drink but may appear up to 7-10 days after the last alcoholic consumption. Over time, symptoms worsen. Once this happens, there are numerous symptoms that afflict the individual. The symptoms include the following.

1. Body tremors.

2. Mental status changes. These problems include:

   a. Agitation, irritability.

   b. Confusion, disorientation.

   c. Decreased attention span.

   d. Decreased mental status. Once mental status is reduced, individuals may experience deep sleep that persists for a day or longer, stupor, sleepiness, or lethargy. These symptoms usually occur after acute symptoms.

   e. Delirium. Individuals who experience delirium experience severe, acute loss of mental functions.

   f. Excitement.

g.   Fear.

h.   Hallucinations. Common hallucinations include seeing or feeling things that are not present. Individuals may see things such as insects, snakes, or rats. They may see these objects or feel like the objects are crawling on their skin.

i.   Highly sensitive to light, sound, or touch.

j.   Increased activity.

k.   Rapid changes in mood.

l.   Excitement and restlessness.

3. Seizures

    a.   The majority of seizures occur within the first 24-48 hours after the last drink.

    b.   These are most common with people who have had previous complications from alcohol withdrawal.

    c.   The seizures are usually generalized tonic-clonic.

4. Symptoms of alcohol withdrawal. These include:

    a.   Anxiety.

    b.   Depression.

    c.   Difficulty with thinking clearly.

    d.   Fatigue.

    e.   Feelings of being jumpy or nervous.

    f.   Shaky feelings.

    g.   Pulsating and general headaches.

    h.   Insomnia.

    i.   Nausea.

    j.   Pale skin.

    k.   Palpitations, which is the sensation of feeling the heart beat.

l. Swift or rapid emotional changes.

m. Profuse sweating, especially on the palms of the hands or face.

n. Vomiting.

o. Fevers, diarrhea, or confusion.

5. Chest pain.

6. Fever.

7. Stomach pain.

8. Rapid muscle tremors.

9. Severe tremors of the extremities.

There are several methods of treatment for delirium tremens. First and foremost, a hospital stay is mandatory. This way, a health care team will be able to regularly monitor the afflicted individual. The team will check blood chemistry results such as electrolyte levels, body fluid levels, and vital signs such as temperature, pulse, rate of breathing, and blood pressure. Once the problem is determined, the appropriate treatment and medications will be made available to the patient. For instance, symptoms such as seizures and heart arrhythmias are treated with medications. The appropriate medications for these health problems include anticonvulsants such as Phenytoin or Phenobarbital, Central nervous system depressants such as Diazepam, Clonidine to reduce cardiovascular symptoms and reduce anxiety, and sedatives. For hallucinating patients, antipsychotic medications must be prescribed. Counseling and support groups are long-term preventive treatments which are a necessity for the success of recovering alcoholics.

Neurotransmitter Change

In order for the brain to function normally, the brain needs to maintain a careful balance of chemicals called neurotransmitters. Neurotransmitters are small molecules, which are involved in the brain's communication system that ultimately help regulate the body's function and behavior. The balances of the neurotransmitter chemicals are altered when alcohol enters the brain. This, in turn, leads to drowsiness, loss of coordination, and euphoria. With ongoing alcohol exposure, the brain begins to adapt to the chemical changes. This happens as a result of the brain compensating for the chemicals in alcohol. With long-term heavy drinking, the brain begins to work to restore its balanced state, which means the task of certain neurotransmitters begins to change in order for the brain to perform normally while alcohol is present. That is why long-term use completely changes the brain's chemistry, which alters an individual's physical and mental health.

As the brain goes through adapting to the prolonged presence of alcohol, a moderate drinker's body will respond differently than the body of one who drinks alcohol heavily. First, alcohol tolerance differs. Those who are heavy drinkers will need to consume more alcohol in order to become intoxicated. Second, moderate drinkers do not have as severe withdrawal symptoms as individuals who drink high amounts of alcohol because of the body's dependence on alcohol. The brain and body start to develop a tolerance and become insensitive to alcohol, which requires heavy drinkers to consume more alcohol to feel its effects. In some cases, high tolerance turns into a dependence on alcohol, meaning the body cannot function properly unless there is alcohol present. The dependent person starts to feel cravings. At this stage of tolerance, once an alcoholic stops drinking, withdrawals become severe. Symptoms of withdrawal include profuse sweating, racing heart rate, and feelings of restlessness and anxiety. Studies have shown that alcoholics who reach this stage of their addictions drink just to avoid the symptoms of withdrawal. Anxiety feelings are even present after the initial withdrawal symptoms have ceased, which is a continuous driving force behind alcohol-use and relapse.

Tolerance and withdrawal are proof that alcohol heavily influences the brain. The brain communicates through a multifaceted system of electrical and chemical signals. Each signal is very important to brain function because it sends messages throughout the entire brain. This, in turn, controls and regulates every aspect of the body's function. The neurotransmitter chemicals are central in the signal transmissions. Once alcohol enters the brain, the balance between the brain and body are disrupted, impairing the brain. For example, the brain balances the activity of inhibitory neurotransmitters, which work to obstruct or end nerve signals, with that of excitatory neurotransmitters, which work to speed up these signals. Alcohol can slow down the signal transmission in the brain, contributing to some of the effects associated with alcohol intoxication, including sleepiness and sedation. Once the brain becomes accustomed the alcohol, it compensates for alcohol's slowing effects by increasing the action of excitatory neurotransmitters, speeding up signal transmission. This way, the brain is able to restore itself to a normal state in the presence of alcohol. If alcohol influence is removed, especially when there is an abrupt halt to alcohol consumption by an addict, the brain most likely will readjust once again. This may possibly lead to unpleasant feelings, which are associated with alcohol withdrawal. Symptoms include "the shakes" or a high level of anxiety.

Genetic Components

With all of the harmful effects that alcohol causes on the body and brain, many ask why are there so many people who abuse alcohol? Studies have shown genetics may play a significant role with alcoholism. Different researchers claim to have identified new genes, which may contribute to excessive alcohol consumption. This may provide clues or answers to the underlying molecular mechanisms and help scientist focus on targets not previously explored in alcohol abuse. Scientists have used several breakthrough study methods, which included using strains of animals that have either high or low inherent preference for alcohol. NIAAA Director Ting-Kai Li, M.D. stated, "These findings provide a wealth of new insights into the molecular determinants of excessive drinking, which could lead to a better understanding of alcoholism. They also underscore the value that animal models bring to the investigation of complex human disorders such as alcohol dependence." Scientists at the University of Texas used microarray techniques to study gene expression in the brain. Through research and tests, the scientists were able to identify nearly 4,000 differentially expressed genes between the high and low alcohol drinking mouse strains and to narrow the focus to 75 primary candidate genes. Also, there were significant comparisons of the mouse data with human genetic studies, which showed that genes with significant expression differences reside in chromosomal regions that beforehand were revealed to be connected with human alcoholism. Dr. Li also stated, "Numerous pathways, as well as genes whose functions are currently unknown, may contribute to the genetic predisposition to drink high amounts of alcohol. Our results will allow us to begin to focus on targets never previously implicated in excessive drinking." The genetic studies researched by NIAAA, which is the National Institute on Alcohol and Alcoholism, have shown that chromosome 9 has genes which may control alcohol consumption in mice. NIAAA's independent analyses permit them to narrow the focus from thousands of genes in that particular region to 20.

Other researchers have used new genomic technology to identify the genes in humans that predispose them for developing alcoholism and who are the most at risk for developing alcoholism. These findings might revolutionize treatment and prevention options. The results have identified clusters of genetic variations in 51 chromosomal regions that are believed to play a role in alcohol addiction through cell-to-cell communication, control of protein synthesis, regulation of development, and cell-to-cell interactions. Although an individual may have a genetic tendency to develop a disease, it does not necessarily mean he or she will have the disease. It only means he or she is at higher risk for doing so than the average person.

The genetic studies have also determined that alcoholism runs in families. This concept is not new, but the study of alcoholism and genetics will help scientists understand the hereditary nature of this disease. Although this particular study has not been completely conclusive, it is on the verge of becoming a breakthrough in determining which families are more susceptible to alcoholism.

In conclusion, the effects of alcohol can lead to devastating consequences on those who abuse or use during pregnancy. Whether participating in binge, social, or addictive drinking, each individual is taking a risk on their physical and psychological health on themselves or others. <u>Although there are studies which have proved the health benefits of moderate wine drinking, all other forms of alcohol consumption only leads to a deterioration of the body and mental functioning.</u>

Chapter 4

DUI Autopsy

How much did you drink on the day of your DUI arrest? (list all the drinks you had that night)

_____
_____
_____

Where did you do the drinking:_____
_____
_____

What were you doing when drinking: _____
_____
_____

Who else was with you, if anyone: _____
_____
_____

What was going on in your life at that time: (Write about your family, significant others, financial concerns, and your job or career, even if you don't think it matters) _____
_____
_____
_____
_____
_____
_____
_____
_____
_____
_____
_____
_____

_____

_____

How were you feeling before you started drinking: _____

_____

_____

_____

How did you feel when you were drinking: _____

_____

_____

_____

Had you planned to drink as much as you did? If you drank more than you wanted list why you think this happened: _____

_____

_____

_____

After drinking, why did you decide to drive: (List all the reasons you can think of why it was alright to drink and drive, list as many as possible) _____

_____

_____

_____

What did you feel like when you were stopped by the police: (List as many feelings you can think of at that time) _____

_____

_____

_____

Thinking back on it, what could you have done differently to have avoided the DUI: (List as many things you can think of that would have changed your behaviors) _____

_____

_____

_____

_____

_____

_____

Do you blame anyone for what happened to you? (i.e., being arrested) Why?

_____

_____

_____

_____

_____

_____

What level of responsibility do you take for your arrest? (1-100%)_____

How often did this behavior happen? (e.g. everyday, once a week, once a month)_____
_____

How honest were you in this Chapter? (1-100%) _____

Chapter 5

WHY DO I MAKE BAD DECISIONS?

Have you ever wondered why you have made poor choices in your life. There are individuals who have a life history of making poor choices. Therapists who have worked with many individuals who have a life history of making poor decisions explain that such individuals all share common factors. In fact, individuals who are least effective in life have the same factors, though they may not have a substance abuse problem but some other method of self destructive behaviors, such as an eating disorder, excessive anger, over-indulging in sex, or gambling.

By this time in your workbook, you will fully understand that thoughts drive emotions and then emotions drive behaviors. What these individuals, described in the previous paragraph, all have in common is a lack of **Modulation**, lack of **Coping Skills**, poor **Problem Solving Skills**, and the **Problem of Instant Gratification**.

The Problem of Instant Gratification (PIG). You may have heard this term before, but this book needs to define Problem of Instant Gratification so we can examine this destructive thought pattern more closely and help make better choices in our lives.

1)   PROBLEM OF INSTANT GRATIFICATION, or (PIG).

Problem of Instant Gratification: Any action or behavior that is to satisfy a negative emotion, where the action is specifically to make ourselves feel better without thinking through the possible negative consequences associated with the action. This behavior can be planned out and not immediate.

What we are really talking about here is the need to feel better now and choosing the fastest easiest way to make ourselves feel better.

For example, individuals often have stress at work, or in the home, and they make a plan to feel better, such as thinking "as soon as I am off work" I am going directly to my favorite bar and unwind. This is an example of PIG. Another example would be at a friend's house after a long and stressful day, and they offer you something to drink, knowing you have no way to get home except for driving yourself. The desire to feel better overcomes the better choice of leaving the situation and saying "not now, but thanks."

2)   MODULATION.

This is worth repeating a hundred times. Modulation is looking at your situation, or any problem, and not thinking the worse possible scenario. Problems in our lives can be overwhelming, and if we want—we can make any problem so overwhelming it sends us into a tailspin. The object is to look at any problem as solvable and not that bad. Again, it's just like the volume control of a stereo. You can look at a problem and crank the problem up to volume "10," or you can crank it down to a "2." It all depends on how you perceive how bad the problem can be. Modulation of our problems and emotions is paramount to being successful in life and not just remaining abstinent from drinking and driving. This concept works at your job, your relationship, and your personal relationship with friends. This concept works in every facet of your life, because the modulation of our emotions affects every aspect of our lives. Do you Ever meet people who are constantly in a state of "drama?" The reason they are in a state of drama is that they are unable to modulate their emotions, and each and every situation becomes overwhelming. Modulating your emotions takes practice so that you can learn to relax and calm down and think things through. The foundation to Modulation is using Coping Skills and better Problem Solving Skills.

3)   IMPUSIVE BEHAVIOR.

Impulsive Behavior: Any physical or verbal reaction to a situation to satisfy a negative emotion without thought of the consequences. This behavior is immediate and not planned out.

Individuals often have no intention of taking any drugs or alcohol, but the moment they are presented with the opportunity, they partake. This can be as simple as an individual walking to his or her car after work and friends are getting "high" in the parking lot.

These concepts, 9(i.e. Problem of Immediate Gratification, Impulsive Behavior, poor Problem Solving Skills, and poor Coping Skills) work hand in hand. The concepts work this way. First, there is a negative emotion, which is derived by an unpleasant thought that instigates the negative emotion. A negative emotion or feeling can also be a continual thing, on a day-to-day basis, such as, "I feel depressed;" "I have anxiety every day;" "I have been physically, sexually, emotionally abused and I can't forget about it;" or "I am in a terrible relationship." Your immediate thought is, "how do I feel better? What can I do to feel better RIGHT NOW or as soon as possible?" This is a very normal human response. We all think the same when we feel terrible or irritated. Remember that a large part of our personal makeup is to seek pleasure and avoid pain. The difference for many is that people with good coping skills and modulation skills handle their problems and negative emotions in a healthy way. They don't chose to drink the problem away, take drugs, go gamble, or some other form of destructive behavior.

This is where the Problem of Immediate Gratification takes place. Next, there is usually some Impulsive Behavior that follows. Many choose to drink or take drugs, as this is an immediate fix for the problem. But the next day the problem is still there, and a continual cycle of poor choices happens over and over. The problem does not go away and usually creates more problems down the road. Eventually, the problems are too overwhelming, and using alcohol to fix the problems just adds more problems to your life.

Many of our actions throughout the day are done quickly and without much thought, and most of these actions or behaviors serve us quite well. It would be difficult to imagine thinking through every one of our actions every day to determine if negative consequences are going to happen. Think for a minute how you get up every morning. If you are like most people, you have a set routine in how to get up each morning. You have formed habits that suit you well, and you don't even have to think about how to take a shower or get dressed in the most efficient manner. These habits would not be considered impulsive as they serve a positive purpose in our lives. Many times, you can be driving down the road and suddenly see a fast food restaurant and pull over to get something to drink, which would not normally be a problem. If you were on the way to a job interview or work, and you pulled over to get a soda that caused you to miss the time for the interview or to show up late for work, this would be called Impulsive Behavior.

The Reason for Impulsive Behavior:

Impulsive behavior is driven by the need to satisfy a negative emotion, most of the time. In general, it is seeking a feeling to make ourselves feel better. Remember that feelings are the same thing as emotions. We often feel bored, lonely, stressed, and the need to seek out something to make ourselves feel better drives the action to do whatever. Often, for many of us, the choice is to take drugs or alcohol. Sometimes individuals choose to eat something, buy something, or engage in sex, for example; but these actions will not satisfy a state of intense anxiety, and that is why drugs or alcohol play such a major role.

We all make bad choices, and it is a learning process to think of the consequences before acting. If you are like many other clients taking this course, hopefully you can recognize a history of doing what feels good at the moment, making poor choices, and not thinking your actions all the way through.

Make a list of 10 things you have done in your life when you acted on an impulse and did not think about the consequences. This would include, as an example, things you have said to your significant other, children, co-workers, friends, buying on impulse, and drinking when you knew there were responsibilities that needed to be met.

1) _____
   _____
   _____

2) _____
   _____
   _____

3) _____
   _____
   _____

4) _____
_____
_____

5) _____
_____
_____

6) _____
_____
_____

7) _____
_____
_____

8) _____
_____
_____

9) _____
_____
_____

10) _____
_____
_____

Now you are going to find out what triggered you to make those choices. Please write down for each one that you have listed, what triggered (i.e. thoughts and emotions) you to make those choices. The reason for this exercise is that you will be able to pinpoint the emotions in you life that drive poor choices. You may find that each poor choice was driven by some common factor, such as stress, anger, frustration, lack of money, relationship problems, low self-esteem, or depression, for example.

1) _____
_____
_____

2) _____
_____
_____

3) _____
_____
_____

4) _____
_____
_____

5) _____
_____
_____

6) _____
_____
_____

7) _____
_____
_____

8) _____
_____
_____

9) _____
_____
_____

10) _____
_____
_____

Now that you have found some impulsive behaviors in your past, and you have been able to identify the negative emotions that drive your poor choices, it's time to find a better solution. These are called **Coping Skills.** I am sure I, and you too, will have some problem this week or month. It never fails, and it will continue the rest of your life. Some of the problems you encounter will be small, and others will feel as if you question the reason for living when problems become overwhelming.

Remember, your perception of "how bad it is" is entirely up to you. If you think the problem is terrible, then it is. If you think it's not a big deal, "I can deal with this," then it's not that big of a problem. Understanding that your perception of a particular problem is the key to controlling your emotions and behaviors. Thinking a particular problem is not that bad can change your feelings instantly: if you don't think the problem is all that bad. The object is for you to recognize the problem and not to react the same way you have in the past. For most of you, the problem solving method was to drink (PIG), to forget about it, and to attempt to deal with it another day. The initial reaction to problems is this overwhelming negative feeling. For each of us it is different. Nevertheless, it is a negative feeling, and we don't like that at all. Again, for most of us, we attempt to use the first thing, or the usual method, to deal with negative emotions. Now it's time to change that.

A **Coping Skill** is to give you time to assess the problem, not react the way you have in the past, and give you time to make the right choice.

List 10 Coping Skills you can realistically use to help alleviate negative feelings. For example, if you feel angry, take a walk outside, listen to music, or go to the gym. Please come up with ideas you feel that will work. You may need help from the group or your therapist. Listen to what other individuals use. Maybe the answer is there.

1) _____
_____
_____

2) _____
_____
_____

3) _____
_____
_____

4) _____
_____
_____

5) _____
_____
_____

6) _____
_____
_____

7) _____
_____
_____

8) _____
_____
_____

9) _____
_____
_____

10)_____

_____

_____

Now, take the list and prioritize the list, place a number by the ones you would use first with the number 1 being the first thing you would use, and the number 10 as the last one you would use. Usually the first 3 are the ones we consider the most useful.

Chapter 6

Pinpointing Your Drinking Triggers

This portion of the program helps pinpoint the circumstances that lead you to drinking outside of the boundaries of moderation. For many of you it is not the situation that creates a drinking and driving problem. It is just another excuse to drink in excess. How often have you heard "the party was great," or "the game was just too exciting and we all got wasted"? If it was not the game or whatever, it would be some other reason to give yourself the justification to drink too much. When you are in social circles, most of you need to justify why you drank heavily, or it would be clear to others you may have a drinking problem. Ever listen to anyone that said "I drank way too much for no reason"? If he or she did say this, surely people would automatically think the person has a drinking problem. Often people find places, situations, and personal things to justify excess drinking. For some of you, it could be the situation that led to your arrest.

Over-drinking situations may involve the following:

- Coping with negative emotion
- Drinking for pleasure
- Drinking from habit in certain situations
- Drinking in excess because the situation gives you the excuse to drink
- Or a mixture of these, in addition to others

Triggers are situations and feelings that involve both the things going on around you and your internal thoughts and feelings. They put us in a mind-frame that "It's time for a drink or to get high."

When you can clearly identify drinking triggers, you can then decide on a better kind of response for the future. The response could involve not drinking, coping with the situation in another way, avoiding that type of situation, or putting a safety plan in place.

- When one of your trigger situations comes up in the future, you can be alert to avoid your old automatic response and instead respond in a more rational and beneficial way.

Triggers for some can include: Timing, Locations, Activities, People Involved, Work Related Circumstances, Financial Related Circumstances, Your Physical State, Relations with Others,

Relationship with Spouse or Significant Other, Parents or In-Laws, Children, Feelings/Emotions, Major Life Events.

Once you isolate the triggers, then you can focus your efforts on finding better ways of handling situations in your life and on behaving in more positive ways.

Pinpointing Your Drinking Triggers

Which trigger areas create the most problem drinking? Rank them from 1 to 5, with 5 being the most occurrences.

- _____ Timing

- _____ Locations

- _____ Activities

- _____ People Involved

- _____ Work-related Circumstances

- _____ Financial-related Circumstances

- _____ Your Physical State

- _____ Relations with Others

- _____ Relationship with Spouse or Significant Other

- _____ Parents or In-Laws

- _____ Children

- _____ Feelings/Emotions

- _____ Major Life Events

- _____ Feeling Stressed/Overwhelmed

- _____ Drinking has always been a part of my life

- _____ I cannot relax and talk to people without drinking

- _____ Other

Use this as a tool to see patterns of drinking. Example: Do most of them involve social occasions, or being alone, or being with family? Are you usually under stress, tired, or in a celebratory mood?

Write a list of your specific triggers by finishing the sentence "I drink . . . ."

Example: I drink when I watch sports, or I drink when I feel stressed.

_____
_____
_____
_____
_____
_____
_____
_____
_____
_____
_____
_____
_____
_____
_____
_____

Plans to Drink Moderately in Trigger Situations

(Remember: for some of you the only thing to do is never drink)

Once you have identified the situations and locations in which you drink or drink in excess, then you can set rules and goals to serve as a plan for managing these situations.

Example:

Situation

Going out somewhere, such as a football party.

What can I say to myself before I get there

I don't need to drink and make a fool of myself or get arrested again. Think about how I want to feel good at work tomorrow and be more productive.

Plan

I will begin the evening by drinking water or soda. I will stick to not having more than 3 drinks all night.

For some of you reading this manual, excess drinking is beyond the situation or the emotions. It can be as simple as. "I drink too much, and I need to stop completely. I understand that I have no control over my drinking, I have tried in the past to stop, but just can't do it on my own." If this is the case for you, the AA program is a great place to start, as controlling the emotions and situations will never be enough once you start drinking.

Exercise: Please write down 4 situations that have caused you to drink in excess. Then make a plan to control your drinking in these situations. You can refer to the Urge Control Skills chapter, and the Drinking Control Skills chapter for help.

#1

Situation:

_____

_____

What can I do or say to myself before I get there?

_____

_____

_____

What is my plan when I get there?

_____

_____

_____

#2

Situation:

_____

_____

What can I do or say to myself before I get there?

_____

_____

_____

What is my plan when I get there?

_____
_____
_____

#3

Situation:

_____
_____

What can I do or say to myself before I get there?

_____
_____
_____

What is my plan when I get there?

_____
_____
_____

#4

Situation:

_____
_____

What can I do or say to myself before I get there?

_____
_____
_____

What is my plan when I get there?

_____
_____
_____

Chapter 7

The D.U.I. Cycle

Every day in our lives, we experience cycles of behavior. A cycle is something that repeats itself over and over due to a set of events or emotions. We create cycles to make our days more comfortable and easier to manage, and then there are some cycles that are destructive to our being. If you examine your day, you will find that you often repeat the same behaviors over and over. You react to the same situations over and over. For example, someone says something negative to you, and the reaction is to say something back to hurt the person. You have a hard day at work, you feel stressed, and the cycle is to drink with your friends, or even worse, by yourself. There are positive cycles in our lives and negative cycles in our lives. Each morning, you get up and find the most efficient way to get your day started. You most likely get dressed the same way, shower the same way, and then out the door you go for other cycles in your life. This serves us well, most of the time. Can you imagine what your life would be like if you had to figure out each morning how to get the day started and get to your job? It would be chaotic and time consuming. If you take a moment and reflect on your daily schedule, you will find numerous things in your life that you repeat over and over.

Cycles can also be considered habits, which can be positive or destructive. Some individuals find they have a habit of smoking a cigarette after each meal, which by today's thinking is a destructive habit. Some have a habit of having a drink as soon as they walk in the door from work. If this was a single glass of wine on occasion after work, then one could consider this a positive cycle of behavior, but this is rarely the case, as we well know. If you are reading this workbook, then you are most likely having problems limiting the amount and how often you drink. As stated in the chapter on Understanding Alcohol Abuse, the use of alcohol releases neurotransmitters that increase the desire to drink more than we would like, and it is difficult to moderate consumption.

The D.U.I. cycle is a chance for you to see how your arrest started and the preceding events that brought you to this point. In other words, it will show you how your behavior started with a set of specific events and negative emotions, leading you to act the way you did. Like others, many often drink and drive after following the same cycle of thoughts and behaviors. As this workbook addressed previously, the "Cycle" starts off with Triggers, which are negative events and emotions that drive poor behaviors and poor decisions. What this chapter will help you learn is some of the events and emotions in your life that lead to your poor decisions. Think about how you react to stressors in your life and events in which you consistently react poorly, such as an argument with a significant other. You will find a pattern to your reactions and behaviors. For example, when there is a problem in a relationship, you may react poorly by shutting down and not talking about the problem. Many people begin raising their voices to be heard, become physically aggressive, break things, or exit the relationship as that appears easier. Maybe at work you feel stressed and argue with others at work. You may feel unable to relax and *not* find a way to communicate the problem in meaningful manner. The next step in the treatment workbook is to help you recognize how you reacted in the past to negative thoughts, feelings, and events. The idea is to find a productive and positive way to cope with negative thoughts to change behaviors.

As you move through treatment you will recognize all of the problems you have been experiencing are interrelated. This means one problem leads to creating problems in other areas of your life. In other words, one problem feeds another problem. A common mistake for most people is thinking that one problem area in their lives does not affect other areas of their lives. This is called **Compartmentalizing.** For example, experiencing a failure in a relationship may lead to feeling fear of starting another relationship. This may lead to isolating oneself from social circles, leading to boredom and loneliness. You may think to yourself that having problems with individuals at work doesn't affect your relationship with your family, but how would it be possible for anyone to come home after a stressful day and be pleasant with the ones they love. How often do we take things out on others when we have a bad day?

Let's get started.

You can use the day of your arrest to complete this chapter, or you can choose another time in your life when you were intoxicated and drove your car while using alcohol/substances to alleviate personal problems.

Triggers

The first part of the cycle is your list of the Triggers usually associated with your drinking. A Trigger is a negative emotion created by a single thought, group of thoughts, or a particular event creating negative emotions. The Trigger, much like the trigger of a gun, sets the cycle in motion. Triggers can be set off by internal thoughts, or external events, but of course this creates negative thoughts even if it starts outside of ourselves. Some of the most common Triggers are: stress, depression, anxiety, feeling inadequate, feeling overwhelmed, unable to solve a particular problem, relationship problems, low self-esteem, a history of sexual or emotional abuse, extended family problems, or financial problems. Often, individuals find that there is not just one Trigger, but much like a soup with a lot of different ingredients, there are many Triggers associated with drinking behaviors. In the first part of this exercise, please list how many Triggers you can think of that affect your life. If you cannot pinpoint your Triggers, how would it be possible to correct your behavior? By understanding the first part of the cycle, the negative thoughts and associated feelings, you can make a plan to alleviate the negative driving forces and find an alternative solution to keep you and others safe. This may very well be the most important part of treatment. At the end of the treatment workbook, you will find a Relapse Prevention Plan outline to help you, but you must understand what feelings need help first. There are some behaviors that are developed over time and are difficult to break as they become a habit, such as drinking after work each day, social circles where drinking is part of the event, or drinking while watching football games on TV, for example. These habits are usually created by negative emotions. Why else would someone drink too much too often? To escape life. To avoid those feelings we do not like.

Triggers

List what Triggers have caused you to drink and drive in the past. What Triggers have caused you to drink too much? (Please list as many as possible).

_____
_____
_____
_____
_____
_____
_____
_____

Describe exactly what you were feeling before you started drinking the night of your arrest.

_____
_____
_____
_____
_____
_____
_____
_____

Did you have a specific plan after you felt like this? Do you have the same or a similar plan when you experience negative feelings?

_____
_____
_____
_____
_____
_____
_____
_____

How did you rationalize you could drink and drive after drinking? Remember Thinking Errors are making something wrong seem right. (List as many Thinking Errors you have used in the past)

_____
_____
_____
_____
_____
_____
_____
_____

Did you promise yourself you would never drink and drive again, if so how often? What did you say to yourself (self promise) to change your behavior the next time?

_____
_____
_____
_____
_____
_____
_____
_____

Problems

List all the problems your D.U.I created for yourself and others in your life. (Please list at least 10 things)

_____
_____
_____
_____
_____
_____
_____
_____

Dealing with Triggers appropriately. (List other ways you can think of to change your Triggers and deal with negative emotions the right way)

_____

_____

_____

_____

_____

_____

_____

_____

Chapter 8

Drinking Control Skills

If You Find Yourself in a Drinking Situation

In each group that you attend, you will find peers who have a serious drinking problem and some peers who have drinking problems to a lesser extent but still have a problem drinking. If you really don't think or don't know what a drinking problem is, then ask your therapist, or read the Chapter on Alcoholics Anonymous. If you find similarities in the testimonial, this is a good indication you have a drinking problem. You may ask yourself if anyone ever told you that you have a drinking problem? Chances are you have heard someone saying you need to moderate or quit drinking.

Again, each of you will determine to what extent you will integrate (i.e. put into practice what you have learned) the material presented in his workbook into your everyday lives. Integration means putting in place the things you have learned from this workbook and treatment concepts presented by your therapist. This workbook and the entire program are absolutely worthless if you don't make changes in your thoughts and behaviors. Each person in the program should be different by the end of the program. If you don't notice a difference in your thoughts and behaviors, you may lack in motivation or self-discipline. The entire program is about a commitment to yourself to improve your life, for yourself, for the community, and for those people you love.

If you want to control your drinking, lessen the amount you drink. If you find yourself in a situation in which you are starting to drink and need more self control, here are some very helpful ideas to give you better self-control.

For many of you, some of these ideas will not be good if you are considered an Alcoholic. Be real with yourself. If drinking has been running and ruining your life, focus on the AA Chapter, and think of joining the AA program. If this is the case, total abstinence is the only way.

Drinking Control Skills

- Begin declining drinks as a habit
- Ask your friends to stop pressing you to have another drink
- Switch to water or soda
- Switch to Non-alcoholic beer
- Eat something until you are full
- Ask the bartender not to serve you
- Give your car keys to a friend
- Give your car keys to a manager
- Send your keys home with a friend who is leaving early
- Leave with a friend who is leaving early
- Have a non-drinking friend take you home (designated driver)
- Call a friend or family member
- Ride a bus
- Call a taxi
- Call a Designated Driver Service (702-456-7433). They will drive you home in your car
- Call a support system member for help or ideas (Example: An AA mentor, someone who knows you are trying to control your drinking habits)
- Discourage yourself from driving by contemplating the consequences
- If possible, get a hotel room where you are

Control Skills for Drinking Situations

1. The First Few Minutes Count

What you do in the first few minutes of a drinking episode can be critical for the way the entire episode unfolds. Have a frame of mind of "moderation and responsibility" before you begin drinking. Attempt to be responsible the entire time you drink. The moments when you first start drinking set the pace for the entire evening. If you start out attempting to just get your "buzz" on as fast as possible, then most likely you will exceed that "buzz" with much more than you intended.

2. Thirst Management

Start with water or soda. Don't begin thirsty. Drink as much water as possible before going out. It's a natural response to drink when we are thirsty, and often it doesn't matter what we drink. It's our body telling us it needs fluids. Always start with water or something you like to drink first when you are at home or away, and you will find your drinking will be much less.

3. Delaying

Show up late. Don't start drinking right away. Walk into any situation and start a conversation first. Look around and see who is there. Look around the room—what's new or different? If you feel some social anxiety, and you need a drink to feel comfortable, stay by a close friend until the anxiety lessens. This is a common phenomenon where individuals feel they need a drink to be social. Learn to be social first and maybe not drink at all.

4. Dilute

Drink beer instead of shots, more orange juice than vodka, more coke than rum. Often people want the drink as strong as possible. Go the other way, and think about drinking more of the fluid than the alcohol. Ask the bartender to make it on the weak side, not "Stiff."

5. Go to a More Expensive Place

Yes, this works. Each time you pay for an overpriced drink, it will ring in your mind that this is ridiculous, and you will enjoy more than indulge.

6. Alternating

Beer then water, then beer again. Drink a beer, and then have a non-alcoholic beer. How about two glasses of water and then a drink?

7. Sipping

Avoid guzzling or chug-drinking. The effects of alcohol can happen quickly, but there is a time delay. How often have you heard of someone saying, "all of a sudden I was hammered, and I'm not sure what happened after"? You can drink more quickly than the alcohol can catch up to you. It builds in your system, and the liver can only process approximately one ounce of alcohol per hour. So if you are drinking too quickly, the odds are it will catch you by surprise.

8. Put the glass down (push the glass as far away as possible)

Keep it out of your hand to reduce the frequency of sips or gulps. Drinking becomes more of a habit with the glass in your hand or nearby. Often you take another sip because it becomes a habit with the drink in your hand. If you push the glass away and have to reach for it each time, you will find that you will drink less. It is amazing how a small thing like this can make a difference in the amount you drink.

9. Planning

Make a conscious decision to space your drinks out or to drink responsibly. Before you go out, have a plan, and stick to it. It is the times we don't have a plan that create those awful nights. Think about only having one drink at the top of the hour. This will help ensure you are not over the legal limit to drive.

10. Self-Talk

Make a conscious decision to space your drinks out or to drink responsibly. Think to yourself throughout the night that, "I am going to maintain myself, and I will not let this situation with the alcohol get the better of me." Continually think about how well you are doing. Be proud of yourself. Focus on that.

11. Focus on the fun

Focus on the conversation or the band that is playing. Think about why you are there. Remember to keep your wits about yourself. No one ever wants to wake up the next morning and think to themselves what a fool they were last night. If you focus on the fun and the people, you will respect yourself the next day, and your friends will invite you back more often. No one wants a drunk at the party, and even bartenders don't want a drunk at the bar. Everyone wants to have fun without drama or worry.

12. Timing

Start a drink at the top of the hour and only on top of the hour. Bring a watch and look at the time. Pace yourself. Don't drink because someone says, "have another." Just simply say, "in a few minutes." Think about drinking one drink an hour, and intersperse that with other beverages that look like an alcoholic drink. Often I have clients who say they feel uncomfortable when people notice they are not drinking. Get a glass of Coke (Pepsi, if they don't have Coke). Put a straw in the glass, and play with the straw. No one will ever know.

13. Think about tomorrow

Remind yourself about how you are going to feel in the morning and how it will impact what you have to accomplish (another day wasted). Can you count the times you were on a diet and drank the night before and attempted to "eat your way out of it?" Maybe you have had to take a Xanax or Valium to get out of the funk. That is no way to live life. Think about getting up and hitting the gym and how much better you look each time you go to the gym instead of "vegging" in front of the TV the next day.

14. Hunger Management

Ever tried to drink after having a huge meal? It's almost impossible for most people. Are you are coming home after work each day and having a drink before eating? Try having a meal that is semi-prepared when you walk in the door, and promise yourself to eat first. You will find the urge to have an alcoholic drink diminishes significantly. Also, have a large glass of something you like to drink with your meal. Eat a large meal before going out. If you think to yourself, "I don't want to eat a large meal because I need to lose weight," just think to yourself that you have a choice to eat some nutritious food or a whole bunch of empty calories by drinking.

Remind yourself of the positives of stopping now or switching to non-alcoholic beverages. List 5 positives for stopping drinking.

_____
_____
_____
_____
_____
_____
_____
_____

List 5 things off of the list of suggestions you will use to limit or help you stop drinking and why they would work for you.

_____
_____
_____
_____
_____
_____
_____
_____

List 5 things off of this list you WOULD NOT USE to limit or help you stop drinking and why they would NOT work for you.

_____
_____
_____
_____
_____
_____
_____
_____

Chapter 9

URGE CONTROL

For the purpose of this book and to maintain simplicity, an "Urge" is defined as a feeling to do a "Negative" behavior, which is to consume a substance to be intoxicated when we know this is the wrong thing to do. An urge is never considered to be positive thing for the purposes of this workbook.

You can have an urge driving down the road to eat or drink something at McDonalds, for example, and for the purposes of this workbook that is not an urge. The feeling that you are thirsty or hungry is not an urge. An urge is considered a thought where there is or can be negative consequences to our behaviors if acted out. If you were to stop to get something to eat when you have an appointment for a job interview, and you have a desire to eat and then miss the job interview, then that would be considered an urge control problem. Of course, you could use a thinking error, such as, "I must have not really wanted the job, or I guess it wasn't meant to be." You can always rationalize why you followed the urge and did not do the right thing. It's easy. You have done it a thousand times. We all have to some extent, some more than others.

For many of you reading this workbook, Urge Control is the main focus of your drinking and driving problem. It is likely you have had other problems in your life where you had urges and you were unable to control your actions, which created other problems in your life. This may be as simple as an urge to tell your boss he is stupid and has no idea what he is doing. Although this may be true, there is a much better answer to this problem than just saying what's on your mind at the time, but if you have little urge control, this is exactly what you might do. In other settings, you may have experienced an urge to buy something fun even when you know your family is struggling financially, and the consequences may be getting into an argument with your significant other when you get home or even being unable to pay your mortgage on time.

<u>The good news is that there are treatment tools you can use to help control urges.</u>

The urge to drink and party with our friends, to go to the local bar when we are bored, or to use any substance comes at us like a wave. An urge is a compelling emotion driven by some underlying feeling of emotional discomfort. An urge is the answer to the underlying negative emotion, and an urge eliminates the negative emotion. The urge itself comforts us and at the same time causes a level of discomfort, as we recognize the urge to do something many of the times has negative consequences. For example, when we are bored, stressed, or lonely, we can have an urge to drink. The urge to drink makes us feel there is a solution to negative emotion, and there is a moment of feeling some relief. Urges are usually brief and at times can seem to haunt us for a good part of the day. Then our thought processes kick in, and most of the time we are able to recognize the negative consequences of those urges, which in itself creates discomfort. Should I drink and party with my friends? Sounds great, but I have no one to take me home and no way to get home. Maybe I should I drive myself. Again, discomfort comes in with the urge. For many of us, the urge wins, and we say, "what the hell? I won't get caught. I will really drive the speed limit and take back roads," or some other wrong thinking.

There is always a constant battle between the urges and thinking errors. If your thinking errors win over the situation, most or all of the time, then you will never have control of your urges. This is how we continually act out on urges. We use thinking errors, which is rationalizing why anything could be a good decision. If we can make an excuse about why our poor decisions are not that bad, then there is no reason for us not to stop the urge. If we can think to ourselves, for example, "life is short, I work hard and I deserve to be free and do what I want. I am not hurting anyone," then why would anyone ever stop acting upon the urge when we just made our urge and behavior seem reasonable? Now it's okay to drink with my friends since, "I won't get caught, because my friends do it all the time and they don't get caught," or "I was just unlucky the last time I got caught."

Sometimes an urge can come from an overwhelming emotion that is positive, for example, winning money, getting a new job, and even falling in love. Emotions drive our behaviors. As you can remember from previous chapters, thoughts create emotions, and our emotions drive our behavior. Most of this workbook focuses on the proven concept that changing our thoughts will change our emotions, which in turn will change our behaviors each and every time.

There are times when an urge is minimal and times when the urge is much larger, like a tidal wave if you will. The frequency and intensity of an urge is different for each of us. Some of us feel as if it goes on all day long, and while those of us who have been working on sobriety for a while have fewer urges each day, none the less, the urge to drink may never completely go away for some of us. The reason that urges continue even for those who have been sober for years is that outside stimuli, which cause urges, come at us in many different shapes and forms. In other words, your outside world influences the way you think and act, which brings on urges to do whatever to feel better. Think about all the media pouring into you each day. As you drive down the road, there are billboards pointing to establishments aimed at having a good time drinking. Think about all the advertisements from the alcohol venders. Aren't they run continuously throughout every football game? How often have you watched a football game, basketball game, and even golf tournament where there have been numerous advertisements about alcohol, good times, parties galore, and beautiful men and women just having a good time. Feel left out at times??? Hanging out with old friends and drinking while telling stories of times when you were younger, when life seemed a bit easier, when you were invulnerable and invincible—who wouldn't want to reminisce about such wonderful experiences over a couple of drinks? How about just finding a way to get rid of the stress of being an adult with a hundred different things you are responsible for and no end in sight? The urge to let all of the stress, boredom, and loneliness go, even for a moment, sounds good doesn't it? Why not just drink and find a way to release the stress? Heck, life is short, so why shouldn't I have a good time while I am alive? What if die next week? There are another hundred reasons to go out and party and not be responsible to anyone, and all of these are thinking errors to make your behavior seem reasonable.

Have there been times in your life when you drove home intoxicated and you thought to yourself how lucky it was that you came home in one piece or did not get arrested? If this has happened to you, then you have experienced urges and thinking errors.

For some of you, there is no moderation in drinking. It's just drink and drink until there is nothing left to drink. This is where the problem lies. Each of us has that one particular thing we have little to no control over. Some of us have no control over gambling, others have no control of eating, spending, drugs, or sex. Most of us have that one thing we know we have less control than we would like to have, and we feel that urge to do whatever too often.

So, how do I control my Urges???

There are several treatment tools you can use to help. Although there are several treatment tools given in this workbook, you will need to pick the tools that works best for you. Everyone is different, and each of us can use what works for us. Remember that one treatment tool is not enough. You should rank and order the treatment tools, think of which tools you like best, and when one tool is not working, go to the next treatment tool. When you are really having a bad day and your favorite treatment tool just is not working and the urge to drink with your friends or wherever is overwhelming, try another option.

List of Treatment Tools to Control Urges.

1. **Think of the Consequences!!!**

   Jail, another blown relationship or job, DUI classes, losing my license, taking the bus everywhere, embarrassing to myself—to my friends—to my co-workers—to my family, cost of increased car insurance, possibly running over some child crossing the street, hitting another car, maybe killing another driver, and etc. When working with clients, I tell them to always remember the most embarrassing moment of their last arrest, and think of that just before they decide to drink.

2. **Aversive Script.**

   This is a technique you can use while you play out your urge in your mind. You have an urge to party somewhere, and the urge becomes more powerful as you think of all the positive things that can come from following your urge. The objective of this technique is to interject a negative consequence into this fantasy of having a good time.

   An urge to get high is accompanied by a fantasy of how much pleasure you will gain if you follow through on the urge to drink. For example, you feel what it's like to be back at the bar, relaxing, talking to your friends, laughing like there is no tomorrow, forgetting about all of your problems. This is exactly why each of us fantasizes about past drinking experiences—because it is pleasurable. We do not have fantasies that are not pleasurable. If it were un-pleasurable or brought up scary thoughts, it would be a nightmare. The objective is to make the fantasy of drinking and letting the good times roll un-pleasurable. This can be done by interjecting negative consequences into the fantasy. Do you remember a very specific moment when you were arrested the first time??? If you are using this workbook, you have had at least one moment when you were totally embarrassed. It may have been standing in front of the judge and people in the court snickering at you, being on the side of the road as other drivers passed by, being in a jail cell, or calling a friend or family member to bail you out of jail. Although this is much like thinking of the consequences, it is not. The object here is to use a specific moment that really hurts you emotionally, such as the previous examples, and put this one moment into your plans. As you are contemplating drinking at the local bar and rationalizing it is alright to drive home from the bar without a designated driver because it is only "just down the road," this is where you would put that embarrassing moment in your thoughts and plans.

3. Empathy.

Think of how your behavior will affect others. It is as simple as that. If you have an urge to drink and drive, or are intoxicated in any way, think of how much this would hurt the people in your life. If I would hurt someone in my car, how would that affect their family, my friends, the people I work with, or my family? If I get another DUI, how will that affect others in my life? Empathy is not something we are born with. It's developed over time. It's when we use it every day in all situations that it becomes stronger. The strength of using empathy in your everyday life is extremely powerful and rewarding.

4. Video Broadcasting.

Video Broadcasting is when you pretend there is a camera on you. You pretend that your significant other, your mother, your sponsor, a mentor, a teacher who helped you in your life, your best friend, or the Police are watching you. As you can reflect upon what these folks are thinking about you, the behavior changes to be more responsible, adult-like behavior.

5. Radio Broadcasting.

This is when you pretend significant others in your life hear your thoughts. This works especially well when you are with someone of importance to you as you are contemplating an urge. You pretend they can hear your urge to get high. This will embarrass you and help take away the urge. How often have you been with someone of importance and planning a way to go and drink? Have there been times when you appeared just fine to a significant other and then you come home drunk? They are completely puzzled as you were just fine that afternoon. Actually you were not. You were planning a drinking experience. They just didn't know it. Remember, urges give us this good feeling, and the embarrassment you create helps wipe out the urge. How grand it would be if you could

51

just tell this person, "I have this urge that is overwhelming me." If you accomplish that, the urge would dissipate.

6. Thought Stopping and Thought Switching.

This is a relatively easy and very effective technique to stop an urge. There is always a thought preceding an urge. You may not always be aware of this as it appears to come out of nowhere. The urge can come from the subconscious, outside stimulus such a TV add, billboard, passing a bar, or even something as simple as a particular smell. As the urge rises up, you need to stop the urge (i.e. the act you are thinking about) by saying to yourself in your mind, or out loud if you are alone, "Stop," and then switch to another thought that is pleasurable. Maybe switch to how nice it feels to be living a sober life rather than being in trouble with the law. If the urge is overwhelming, you can scream "Stop!" Just find a place no one near will hear you, such as a car with the windows rolled up. You don't want to be taken away as a nut case, LOL. Many clients do scream, and the release of emotions works well to get rid of any urge.

7. Stay Busy.

This is also extremely effective in stopping urges and controlling our behaviors. So often, we drink and party wherever out of boredom. If you feel an urge is overwhelming, just find something to do that is fun. Find anything to take your mind off the urge. Just getting up and starting something is enough to fight off an urge, as urges are usually short-lived. At first, while attempting to live a sober lifestyle, the urge to get high, get that buzz, or have a good time is present throughout the day, but as time passes, the urges become smaller and less frequent. The object is to have several things to do that you really enjoy. Pick some hobbies, read a book, write a book, call your support friends, or surf the net. How about exercise? OMG, lose weight, get in shape, look better, feel better, build self-esteem, doesn't that sound terrible?

8. Aversion Therapy.

This technique is to pair a pleasurable thought, such as getting high, with an un-pleasurable smell or general pain. This technique has been used with several different disorders and works quite well, but usually people don't follow through as it creates discomfort. For an example of how this works, can you remember the time you first smelled cut grass, and then you remember a specific time, place, and the age you remembered this smell? Absolutely—a smell can retrieve memories, which may be good or bad. As from before, an urge is pleasurable, and the objective here is to pair a pleasurable urge with an unpleasant smell. If you are having extreme urges to drink, you can use ammonia snap caps at this time. The pain associated with the urge eliminates the urge. In the future, if the urge comes up again, your brain will remember the pain associated with the urge, and the urge will be cancelled out. This is difficult to follow through and takes some real effort on your part if you choose to do it. Remember to contact your physician to make sure this is not harmful to you, as you may have some physical problems associated with this technique. Another method is to smell Fox Urine, which is available at most sporting goods stores. Fox urine is particularly nasty, very nasty in fact. The object is, as you take a drink, you smell fox urine at the same time. It pairs the smell of alcohol with the fox urine, and each time you drink, the smell comes back and eliminates the desire to drink.

9. **Medication Management.**

There are some medications that reduce the urge to drink and work very well. This may be the easiest way to reduce the urge to drink and control drinking. If you find the other techniques are not working well, make an appointment to see a medical doctor and get a prescription. There are 3 medications approved for helping individuals to stop drinking. One of the medications is Antabuse. This medication will make you sick to your stomach with just one drink, and many people will throw up after one drink. The other 2 medications on the market is Naltrexone and Nalmefone, which are inhibitors to stop drinking by lessening the urge to drink. According to the experience of clients on this medication, they sometimes drink, but much less. Speak to your doctor about the appropriate medication for you before attempting to take anything.

Urge Control Assignments.

1. **List 5 negative consequences you can think of _NOT_ listed in this chapter if you were to get another DUI.**

   _____
   _____
   _____
   _____
   _____
   _____

2. **To use Aversive Script, what 3 things would you use, in order of importance, to help you control your thoughts and urges?**

   _____
   _____
   _____
   _____
   _____
   _____

3. **List 5 different people in your life who would be affected by you getting another DUI. Write their first names, and write how you think a DIU again would affect them.**

   _____
   _____

_____
_____
_____
_____

4. If you were to use Video Broadcasting, who would you use to be watching you? List 3 people, give their first name, and list why you would choose these people to be watching.

_____
_____
_____
_____
_____
_____
_____

5. If you were to use Radio Broadcasting, what thoughts would you broadcast? List 5 things that would be embarrassing to you and the person listening.

_____
_____
_____
_____
_____
_____
_____

6. List 5 things you can do to stay busy that you enjoy and why they would work.

_____
_____
_____
_____
_____
_____

7. Write if you think Aversion therapy is something you would use. Write why or why not.

_____
_____
_____
_____
_____
_____

8. Write if you would consider seeking a medical review for medication. Write why or why not.

    _____
    _____
    _____
    _____
    _____
    _____

9. Write down the name of a physician and the phone number, even if you would never contact a physician for these medications.

Doctor's Name:

_____

Phone Number:

_____

Chapter 10

EMBARRASSMENT

"I will never do anything again that will embarrass myself, my family, or my friends"

This is a very powerful statement or motto and can be life transforming. If you were to follow this one statement, you would not need the rest of this book or maybe any other workbook. Embarrassment is a learning tool we all use to change our behaviors, and it is something to be avoided. When it occurs, change can take place, but do we really have to go through embarrassment to change?

If you were to live by this one motto and no other motto, your life would be rewarding on a personal level. If you don't do anything to embarrass yourself or others, then you are being productive, considerate, kind, motivated, thinking about the feelings of others, and helping others (not helping someone that needs help is embarrassing as well).

Therefore, it is important to instill this value in your life. One of the best ways to instill this value is by repetition of the saying. If you are motivated enough (which you should be) make a banner with this saying and place it on a wall in your home. Write it out and place it on the refrigerator or place it on the back of your bedroom door. The benefits of this saying and living this motto on a daily basis is truly life transforming.

Write down what Embarrassment you experienced by being arrested, describe your feelings. (If you did not feel Embarrassment write down why you did not feel any Embarrassment) _____

_____

_____

_____

_____

_____

_____

_____

_____

_____

_____

For the next 3 days write down 10 times a day, "I will never do anything again to Embarrass myself, my family, or my friends."

Day One:

_____

_____

_____

_____

_____

_____

_____

_____

_____

_____

_____

_____

_____

_____

_____

_____

_____

_____

Day 2:

_____

_____

_____

_____

_____

_____

_____

_____

_____

_____

_____

_____

_____

_____

_____

_____
_____
_____

Day 3:

_____
_____
_____
_____
_____
_____
_____
_____
_____
_____
_____
_____
_____
_____
_____
_____
_____
_____
_____
_____
_____
_____

Did You Start Your Banner???

Chapter 11

The Apology Letter

It is time to write an apology letter. The reason to write an apology letter is to take accountability for your behavior. Without taking accountability for your actions why would you ever change? The first step in change is recognizing there is a problem and your behaviors can hurt yourself and others. Writing the apology letter will help you clarify there is a problem and you are willing to change, and you feel remorse for what did happen or could have happened to someone else. Without doubt your behavior has harmed or embarrassed the people around you. Possibly by the worry you created, or the financial problems being arrested has caused for the love ones around you.

Often individuals feel the only person hurt was themselves. If you feel this way, chances are you are not willing to change your behaviors. People can justify that no one else was hurt by all of this but themselves. There was no accident, I was very careful, and I was driving safely. Some individuals even say they drive well when intoxicated. This makes sense to many people found driving under the influence. But then again, there are those cases, way too many in fact, where some kid on a bike crosses the street without looking or something similar, and if a person is impaired the worst possible things can happen. Approximately 38 people a day die from drunk drivers on the roads. You can count yourself lucky if you did not injure another human being. Far too often drinking and driving directly injures others. You are responsible for the safety of yourself, people in the community, neighbors, and your family. The effect of your behavior being arrested did affect you, your family, friends, people at work, and everyone you know. Your arrest affected all the people you know, and you embarrassed yourself and them.

Your therapist may want you to have a significant other sign off on the apology letter, maybe you feel giving this letter to someone who cares about you can help heal your relationship, and give them hope your poor choice will not happen again. Presenting this letter to the significant relationships in your life will help others in your life feel better about you.

Here is the guide for writing your apology letter. Follow the steps below and sign the apology letter, also have someone in your family, or friend sign the letter as well. This is part of taking accountability for your behaviors.

Apology letter guide:(Write this out on a separate piece of paper, and read it to your therapist or group peers. The Apology Letter should be at least 2 pages).

1) Make a meaningful greeting to all individuals in your life that were effected by your D.U.I.

2) Apologize to them, and state how sorry you are for your behaviors.

3) Make a statement of responsibility for your behaviors. Please do not blame anyone for your behavior. For example, telling a significant other that if they did not argue with you that day this would have never happened.

4) Explain to them they have the right to be mad at you, and it's alright if they express anger, sadness, or disappointment in you.

5) Explain in the letter exactly what you did that day that led to your arrest. Speak to how you made a bad decision, not an excuse for the behavior.

6) Explain how your behaviors may have hurt them. Use empathy and list as many different ways you can think of how your behaviors affected them.

7) Include in this that no one else is responsible for your actions.

8) Explain how treatment is helping you, and what you plan to change in your life to ensure that this will never happen again.

9) Apologize one more time for your behaviors.

10) Sign and date the Apology Letter, then have another person sign off as well.

Chapter 12

ALCOHOLICS ANONYMOUS

This chapter was written for those individuals that want to stop drinking completely. This program has proven over time to be one of the most effective ways to control excess alcohol consumption. This program has changed the lives of many individuals. You may want to refer back to the Testimonial after your read this chapter.

Alcoholics Anonymous was founded in June 1935 by a New York Stockbroker named Bill W. and an Akron Physician, Dr. Bob, when one recovering alcoholic, Bill W., decided to share his experience, strength, and hope with another drunk, not yet sober. Its founding premise, that one alcoholic talking to another can help where nothing else can, was born and the idea soon flourished. This is the key, members believe, that help to make the program so successful, along with these "three pertinent ideas:

a) That we were alcoholic and could not manage our own lives.

b) That probably no human power could have relieved our alcoholism.

c) That God could and would if He were sought."[1]

It appears to work where many other methods have failed.

Alcoholics Anonymous is not a cult, nor is it a religion. It is simply a Fellowship consisting of recovering alcoholics and those who wish to recover. Here is their preamble:

"Alcoholics Anonymous is a fellowship of men and women who share their experience, strength and hope with each other that they may solve their common problem and help others to recover from alcoholism.

---

1   "Alcoholics Anonymous," Page 60

- The only requirement for membership is a desire to stop drinking. There are no dues or fees for A.A. membership; we are self-supporting through our own contributions.
- A.A. is not allied with any sect, denomination, politics, organization or institution; does not wish to engage in any controversy; neither endorses nor opposes any causes.
- Our primary purpose is to stay sober and help other alcoholics to achieve sobriety." [2]

Alcoholics Anonymous is a program based on attraction rather than promotion. The group and its individuals do not go out and recruit new members, and everyone is welcome. Within the Fellowship, one can find men and women of all ages, young and old, all levels of social and economic standings, and numerous cultural and religious backgrounds. But that is not what defines a person here. It is the shared disease of alcoholism—a mental obsession focused on having to drink, and a physical allergy that keeps them drinking once they've started. Contrary to popular belief, alcoholics have just as much willpower and a desire to quit as the next person; what they have lost is the choice whether or not to drink. Due to this obsession and physical allergy which causes them to be unable to stop once they've started, the life of an alcoholic is a tortuous one—for them and for those around them, including spouses, children, family members, employers, and friends.

Unfortunately, there is no one clear definition of alcoholism and no one clear pattern. Some have lost everything from their families, to their homes, to their jobs, and some continue functioning and have lost only those intangible things like self-respect, self-worth, and self-identity. And still others have lost their freedom, either by being institutionalized or imprisoned. Either way, once they have hit rock bottom, they finally are able to now possess the desire to want to stop drinking.

No one in A.A. can actually say why a set of circumstances worked this time, when they were identical just years before. A popular saying within the Program is, "We are ready, when we are ready; we hear, when we hear." Another one is, "When the student is ready, the teacher appears." There are many well-known clichés and one-liners within this spiritually-based Fellowship from "one day at a time" to "easy does it, but do it." It is a Program that teaches alcoholics how to live without alcohol. To an alcoholic, alcohol is the solution, not the problem. But in all actuality, the problem is life—alcoholics tend to have a living problem and so they drink to be able to function and manage and deal with reality. And their perception of reality is askew—the minds of the alcoholic are not that of normal men and women. People with alcoholism tend to be overly sensitive, child-like, immature, irresponsible, and have what is called a "magnifying mind," which tends to focus on the negative and places blame on outside people and issues instead of being accountable for themselves. Alcoholics Anonymous seems to teach those with these particular difficulties how to live not only without drinking, but also, how to live successfully by handling life's daily challenges. It is all about change and contrary action—from not hanging out at the bars or with our friends who drink to doing exactly the opposite of what their ill minds tell them to do. For example, an alcoholic might have a grand idea not to go to their meeting, which is exactly what they need to do; they might not want to go to work, but learn to do so, on a daily basis. Or they might not like a coworker and instead of saying what is on their minds, they smile and treat that person with the respect that they would want.

Alcoholics learn to do these things, and so much more, by working the Twelve Steps of Alcoholics Anonymous, by going to meetings regularly, by practicing the principles of the Fellowship in all areas of their lives, by giving of themselves to others, whether fellow alcoholic or not, and by learning to have a faith and trust in a Higher Power. All of these things sound simple, but they are not easy. There is so much more to quitting drinking than just not drinking. There is a whole new life out there to be lived. Alcoholics Anonymous is like "Life 101"—a classroom where one can be among his literal peers, those people who really know how he thinks, feels, acts, and behaves, and who teaches the newcomer how to live life successfully without the crutch of the drink and the pitfalls that come with it.

Following are The Twelve Steps of Alcoholics Anonymous:

1. We admitted we were powerless over alcohol—that our lives had become unmanageable.

2. Came to believe that a Power greater than ourselves could restore us to sanity.

3. Made a decision to turn our will and our lives over to the care of God *as we understood Him*.

4. Made a searching and fearless moral inventory of ourselves.

5. Admitted to God, to ourselves and to another human being the exact nature of our wrongs.

6. Were entirely ready to have God remove all these defects of character.

7. Humbly asked Him to remove our shortcomings.

8. Made a list of all persons we had harmed, and became willing to make amends to them all.

9. Made direct amends to such people wherever possible, except when to do so would injure them or others.

10. Continued to take personal inventory and when we were wrong promptly admitted it.

11. Sought through prayer and meditation to improve our conscious contact with God *as we understood Him*, praying only for knowledge of His will for us and the power to carry that out.

12. Having had a spiritual awakening as the result of these steps, we tried to carry this message to alcoholics, and to practice these principles in all our affairs.[3]

---

3   "Alcoholics Anonymous," Page 59-60

Believe it or not, most alcoholics have to pause here and seriously contemplate their options . . . . work the twelve steps listed above, or continue on down the path to insanity and death. This is not an easy choice. But before any of these Twelve Steps can be taken and for a sober life to be found, an alcoholic must first take the first step in recovery and that is to "to fully concede to our innermost selves that we were alcoholics." [4]

The most important word within this program is the first word in the first step, "We." To members it means many things from never having to go through anything alone, and knowing there are others who think and feel just like they do, to finally believing that they need to rely on others and a Higher Power to stay sober.

Alcoholism is a progressive disease. It always gets worse, never better. Alcoholics Anonymous is a recovery program that teaches you how to live without drinking and gives alcoholics a newfound freedom. Instead of feeling deprived or feeling like their lives are over, in A.A., alcoholics finally feel like life has just begun.

The main text within this worldwide Fellowship is the book, "Alcoholics Anonymous," commonly called the "Big Book." Within the pages is found a widely accepted definition of alcoholism as a disease and a detailed description of the problem. More importantly, within the first one hundred and sixty-four pages written by its co-founder Bill W. and the first one hundred recovering alcoholics, is found the solution to how they recovered, and specifically, what an alcoholic can do today to recover, as well.

Another widely used text within the A.A. program is called, "Twelve Steps and Twelve Traditions," written by Bill W. in 1952. Within this text there are twelve chapters, one for each step, which goes into more explanation and detail on what is to be done for each individual step. The second-half of the book contains twelve more chapters giving the history of how each of the twelve traditions of the program were created and formed. These are particularly important to show how A.A. really works and how an unorganized organization can still survive in today's societies.

There are also numerous pamphlets, usually free, that describe in detail a multitude of topics from "44 Questions" to ask yourself to help discover whether or not you may be alcoholic, to "This is A.A., an Introduction to the A.A. Recovery Program," and everything in between.

The Big Book of "Alcoholics Anonymous," the "Twelve Steps and Twelve Traditions," along with several other A.A. approved literature can be found in most local libraries and at book stores. To find local meetings or a nearby A.A. office, one can look up A.A. listings in the telephone book; Also online at *www.aa.org*. Or you can write to the world service office at:

> General Service Office
> Box 459, Grand Central Station
> New York, NY 10163

---

[4]   "Alcoholics Anonymous," Page 30

Anyone who contacts their local A.A. office or the General Service Office in New York can be certain of his or her anonymity, one of the other important factors of this program's success.

Once anyone contacts their local service office to get listings of neighboring groups, they can begin going to meetings and seeing where they feel most comfortable. Members say to look for the similarities and not the differences, keep an open mind, and attend a weekly meeting at least three times before discarding it and picking out another group. There are two main types of meetings, "open meetings" and "closed meetings." "Open meetings" are basically open to anyone, whether they have already decided they are alcoholic, or still unsure, or anyone interested in A.A. is also welcome to attend these meetings. Here, speakers share what it was like, what happened to them, and what it is like now that they've found A.A. "Closed meetings" are for alcoholics only, where members share openly in a group setting on problems with living life sober or challenges they may be currently dealing with. Other experienced A.A. members can also offer solutions on how they had dealt with these same issues either by using the Twelve Steps or other "spiritual tools" of the program.

Within these groups is found a Fellowship unlike any other. Here, recovering alcoholics and those wanting to recover, can find true friendship and brotherhood and a place of belonging where none existed before. There is a sense of relating and understanding within these groups that alcoholics had seemed to search for unsuccessfully their entire lives before entering the rooms of A.A. Anyone entering a meeting will see a sparkle in the eyes of recovering alcoholics and a smile on their faces where dread and horror used to exist. A true transformation has taken place in the lives of the members of Alcoholics Anonymous and it is a wonder to behold. Hugs and warm welcomes are a popular form of expressing acceptance and fondness to fellow members and newcomers alike. People who were once selfish, self-centered, and self-absorbed now extend their hands and arms out to those who are suffering. And sober members will continue to perform acts of kindness to friends and fellow members, extending what was so freely given to them. Recovering alcoholics in A.A. soon discover a spirit of giving and love and friendship that they had sought for their entire lives.

There is a newfound freedom, a joyful heart, and a new way of living where once was misery, depression, and despair. Here, the hopeless find hope and the bewildered find guidance and tools to recovery. The lonely find a multitude of friends and a new purpose for living. Here is what is known as "The Promises" in this wondrous Fellowship that can be obtained through working the Twelve Steps:

"If we are painstaking about this phase of our development, we will be amazed before we are halfway through. We are going to know a new freedom and a new happiness. We will not regret the past nor wish to shut the door on it. We will comprehend the word serenity and we will know peace. No matter how far down the scale we have gone, we will see how our experience can benefit others. That feeling of uselessness and self-pity will disappear. We will lose interest in selfish things and gain interest in our fellows. Self-seeking will slip away. Our whole attitude and outlook upon life will change. Fear of people and of economic insecurity will leave us. We will intuitively know how to handle situations which used to baffle us. We will suddenly realize that God is doing for us what we could not do for ourselves.

Are these extravagant promises? We think not. They are being fulfilled among us—sometimes quickly, sometimes slowly. They will always materialize if we work for them." [5]

Bibliography

Anonymous, Alcoholics (1976). *Alcoholics Anonymous* (Third Edition ed.). New York: Alcoholics Anonymous World Services.

Anonymous, Alcoholics (1984). *This Is A.A.* New York: Alcoholics Anonymous World Services.

---

[5] "Alcoholics Anonymous," Pages 83-84

Chapter 13

A Relapse Prevention Plan

It is time to develop your Relapse Prevention Plan. This is your plan to help you maintain your behaviors in high risk situations. You will be able to identify and recognize high risk situations and use Avoidance Strategies and Escape Strategies. You will list coping skills to control urges and lapses, and counteract thinking errors that may lead you to driving under the influence again. The most important idea is to list the treatment tools you have learned that work for you. If you don't think a particular skill works for you, don't list it. You are asked to list several treatment concepts for each part, but for some of you only a few solid concepts can make the difference, if you apply the concepts on a consistent basis.

The Re-Arrest Chain

Before beginning the Relapse Prevention Plan, it is important to discuss and understand the Re-arrest Chain. The <u>Re-Arrest Chain</u> is a fairly specific chain of events each individual goes through before being arrested again. There are five steps each person usually goes through before being arrested again, or driving while intoxicated. As any normal day unfolds, it is doubtful that anyone would think to themselves "I am going to get arrested tonight." In almost all situations there are circumstances that lead to an individual being arrested again. It is your job to recognize the many different circumstances and thinking that lead to drinking and driving. Here is the general order many people follow the day of drinking while driving. Each phase leads a person closer and closer to being arrested again.

Re-Arrest Chain

1) Triggers (Personal Stressors)

2) Unimportant Situations

3) High Risk Places

4) Lapse (Urge to drink)

5) Thinking Errors

6) Giving In

7) Relapse (Driving under the influence)

Here is an example of the Re-Arrest Chain. John who has been abstinent from drinking for several years is driving his car down the road after work with his friend. It's been a long day and both men are tired, but feel pretty good about the week, and glad it's over. John has been stressed recently because even though he has been working steadily he is still behind on his bills. John's friend asks John to pull over at bar so that he can cash his check, which is called an **Unimportant Decision**. It appears to be an unimportant decision as John has no intention of drinking. He thinks to himself being in the bar for a few minutes is no big deal. Once inside the bar John has now placed himself in a **Dangerous Situation**. He is now in a bar feeling relieved the week is over and still stressed from his financial problems. Stress has been one of John's Triggers, and he has usually dealt with stress in the past by drinking. As John is looking around the bar he starts to **Lapse**. John has the Urge to drink. This is where he is thinking about having just one drink. He notices all the people in the bar having a good time, relaxed, and enjoying life the way he did at one time. John starts to have **Thinking Errors** (remember, a thinking error is making something wrong seem right). He says to himself, I can have one drink, that's no big deal. I remember many times I had one drink and stopped; one drink never hurt anyone. I only live a mile away, even if I do have a couple of drinks I am so close to home. It's been almost 2 years and I can control myself much better now. I will have one drink, and it will be a beer, that's not bad, my wife will understand. Beer is not like hard alcohol. I will be under the legal limit. I will drive home slowly, and I won't hurt anyone. John is now at the **Giving In Stage**. This is where John has his first drink, and decides he can control his drinking. This is a huge Thinking Error. What makes John think he control himself on this day, when he had problems controlling his drinking throughout his life? After a while he has another drink, and starts having fun with his new friends at the bar. John decides to have a couple of shots with his new friends. John becomes the life of the bar, which was usually the case after he had a few drinks. John also missed being the center of attention, now he was the life of the party again, even after most of the people he started drinking with had left the bar some time ago.

Somewhere during this time John realizes he has had too much to drink. His friend has had more to drink than John, not that his friend wanted to go anywhere else as this was just too much fun to leave. John starts to think about what his wife is going to say about being late, drinking, and spending money they don't have to take a taxi home. John thinks to himself how embarrassing it would be to call his friends for a ride, because he promised them he would never drink again. John thought about calling his wife for a ride home, but decided a couple of breathe mints and he could pull this off by going home and straight to bed. John rationalized it was only 7 PM and most of the cops are not on the road yet, he felt fairly safe he could make it home without problems, as long as he drove home slowly. John decides to leave the bar, get in his car, and head home (**Relapse**).

John gets into his car and makes sure he is buckled up, sits up straight, looks straight ahead to make sure an Officer would not have a reason to pull him over. John ends up getting arrested again. As John was driving home as safe as possible he was hit from behind while stopped at a red light. In a furious rage John jumps out of the car and starts yelling at the man in the car behind him. Unbeknownst to John was the man was much bigger and had a very bad temper. In an intoxicated state of mind just realizes the trouble he is in and explodes with a verbal assault. The other man proceeded to knock John unconscious, and left the scene of the accident. John laid on the ground unconscious while other drivers stopped to help. Just then a police car happened by and stopped. When the officer finally got John to his feet he realized John was intoxicated and arrested him. John's car was wrecked, he had to go to the hospital, he was fired for missing work, and back to jail for his second DUI.

This was a true story. The name was changed and other details to protect the person's identity.

John had no idea how one small Unimportant Decision could get him arrested AGAIN.

We could have put down a hundred ways John could have been pulled over and arrested again. The biggest thinking Error of all was thinking "I won't get caught." There is an old saying which is fairly wise. If you can think of 50 ways to avoid being caught you are a genius, but there are always a 100 ways to get caught. The moral of this saying is that no matter how many ways you think you can avoid being arrested again, there are still another 50 ways you have not even thought about. That is the truth, and it is something that has been proven over time by thousands of people.

There are those individuals that choose to drink too much the night of their arrest. Most likely it was due to stressors in your life and drinking has been a way to handle problems and relieve stress. If this is the case for you, focus on coping skills to alleviate stress in your plan. If you eliminate stressors in an appropriate manner, the odds are you have a much better chance of dealing with your problems the right way. If drinking has been a problem throughout your life, please think about total abstinence. Please think about the AA program and gain the help of a sponsor. Maybe it's a good idea to read the testimonial again. Maybe it's a good idea to ask your friends if they think you have a drinking problem. It's a good idea for everyone reading his manual to think about all the destructive behaviors and consequences alcohol has brought into your life.

The objective of your Relapse Prevention Plan is to avoid each step of the Re-Arrest Chain and make better choices to avoid being arrested for another DUI.

The first step is to recognize when you are at High Risk to be tempted to Drink and Drive. This step is exactly like the Offense Cycle from a previous chapter, and it is essential you know your triggers well, so you are especially aware of when you need to be more cautious.

List 5 Triggers of significance. Please don't look back at your previous work, you should know these by heart. Triggers are negative emotions that enable us to make poor choices and justify poor behaviors. Remember, you are at the highest risk when you don't feel good about yourself, your life, and you feel life is out of control.

My Triggers Are:

1)_____
_____

2)_____
_____

3)_____
_____

4)_____
_____

5)_____
_____

To avoid moving down the Re-Arrest Chain, how will you alleviate those Triggers before the problems become too much to handle. For example, if one of my triggers is Stress, write down some of the things you have learned in treatment to handle stress in an appropriate manner. You can put down more than 5 Triggers if need be, and for each one of your Triggers you should have a treatment tool to help (i.e. coping skill). If you are not sure how to alleviate a specific Trigger that your counselor may not have gone over in class, just ask for some help. There are some Triggers where you will need to put down several coping skills. As you have learned, coping skills only work if they apply to the situation. For example, if working out is your coping skill for stress, it may not be possible if it is freezing outside and late at night. You will need to have several coping skills for different situations.

For each one of your negative emotions write down some coping skill to each negative emotion. For some of you, it's the urge to drink. Write how you will eliminate the urge.

1) My Negative Emotion is:

_____

I will resolve this negative feeling by:

_____
_____
_____
_____

2) My Negative Emotion is:

_____

I will resolve this negative feeling by:

_____
_____
_____
_____

3) My Negative Emotion is:

_____

I will resolve this negative feeling by:

_____
_____
_____
_____

4) My Negative Emotion is:

_____

I will resolve this negative feeling by:

_____
_____
_____
_____

5) My Negative Emotion is:

_____

I will resolve this negative feeling by:

_____
_____
_____
_____

Now you can help yourself eliminate urges and negative emotions by yourself, and with the help of your support team. Most people find they need the help of friends and family to be successful, don't forget to add this to your plan.

To be completely safe, it is very important not to put yourself in a situation which could compel you to drink again. If you were asked to go with someone to a place you know may cause problems (i.e. High Risk places, such as a favorite bar or with friends that drink) how would you get out of that situation? List 4 things you could say or do to Avoid being in a high risk situation or make an Unimportant Decision.

1) _____
_____

2) _____
_____

3) _____
_____

4) _____
_____

Great!! Now that you have that under control, what would you say or do to get out of a risky situation (i.e. High Risk Situation)? Maybe a place you know there is peer pressure to drink? Maybe a place you found yourself drinking much of the time before you were arrested.

List 4 things you could say or do to get you out of a High Risk Situation.

1) _____
_____

2) _____
_____

3) _____
_____

4) _____
_____

For whatever reason, you find yourself in a high risk situation that is difficult to avoid. This could be a company barbeque, or a wedding with old friends that like to "party" all the time for example. You don't want to leave early or not attend, as leaving or not attending may ruin some relationships. During this time you start to Lapse (i.e. the urge to have a drink) and you find yourself using thinking Errors (e.g. I won't get caught, one or two drinks wont' be bad, I can control my drinking). Remember Lapsing is thinking about having the first drink? Thinking Errors are justifying why it is ok to drink. List 5 treatment tools in this workbook you have learned to control a Lapse or the Urge to drink.

1.) _____
_____

2) _____
_____

3) _____
_____

4) _____
_____

5) _____
_____

Great!! Now you have options to control the urge to drink and drive. But we still have to overcome the Thinking Errors that can get in the way of being successful. Thinking Errors fight against the logic of urge control skills. For example, "I live right down the street, I won't get caught. I have gotten away with this plenty of times in the past." Now, list 5 thinking Errors you have used in the past to justify why it was alright for you to drink drive. List what your thinking Errors have been, and what will you do differently when a Thinking Error occurs.

1) My Thinking Error is:

_____

I will resolve this Thinking Error by:

_____
_____
_____
_____

2) My Thinking Error is:

_____
_____

I will stop this Thinking Error by:

_____
_____
_____
_____

3) My Thinking Error is:

_____

I will resolve this Thinking Error by:

_____

_____

_____

_____

4) My Thinking Error is:

_____

I will resolve this Thinking Error by:

_____

_____

_____

_____

5) My Thinking Error is:

_____

I will resolve this Thinking Error by:

_____

_____

_____

_____

Even better now, you have a good grasp on how to handle your negative emotions better, you will not place yourself in risky situations, and if you do find yourself in a risky situation you can use these skills to keep you safe, and other safe.

Now, what if you get to the point you find yourself at the Giving In Stage? List 5 things you can do to help yourself to get out of this situation?

1) _____

_____

2) _____

_____

3) _____

_____

4) _____
_____

5) _____
_____

There are some of you that will stumble and fall back into drinking while in possession of your vehicle (i.e. No designated driver). The question is, what choice will you make to Not Drink and Drive Again? Please don't list sleeping in your car. Having possession of your keys in or around the car can lead you to being arrested. List 5 things you will do if you find yourself in this situation.

1) _____
_____

2) _____
_____

3) _____
_____

4) _____
_____

5) _____
_____

FANTASTIC!!!! You now have a solid plan to keep you safe from every being arrested again, and keep those you love and those you don't know safe as well.

Here is the final outline for you to complete. Please do a good job by writing neatly, as this plan is the key to changing your life.

Keep this plan somewhere you can see it once in awhile. Place it on the refrigerator door, in a drawer you open up often, the back of a door to a bedroom. Don't place it where you will not see it from time to time, as you have to remember as time passes the rate of relapse goes up as we forget all that you have been through.

If you do all of these things, and remember the treatment Motto "I will never do anything to Embarrass Myself, My Family, or My Friends" you should be just fine. Really enjoy life without being intoxicated, and especially Never Driving Under the Influence.

My Safety Plan

Describe what was happening to you emotionally at the time of your arrest and what needs and emotions you were trying to satisfy. Tell your Therapist or group peers how you will

satisfy those needs in the future without Drinking and Driving again. Write down a plan to keep yourself safe, sign it, and give a copy to your Therapist for approval.

RELAPSE PREVENTION PLAN

FOR: _____

1) What was I feeling and what were my behaviors like before I was arrested for Drinking and Driving?

   _____
   _____
   _____
   _____
   _____

2) What will I do if I feel that way again, how will I alleviate negative emotions?

   a)_____
   _____

   b)_____
   _____

   c)_____
   _____

   d)_____
   _____

3) What I will do if I am asked to do something which is a Seemingly Unimportant Decision, and could place me in a High Risk Situation?

   a) _____

   b) _____

   c) _____

   d) _____

4) What will I do if I find myself in a High Risk Situation?

   a) _____

   b) _____

c) _____

d) _____

5) What I will do if I Lapse or start to use Thinking Errors?

    a) _____

    b) _____

    c) _____

    d) _____

6) What I will do if I get to the Giving In Stage?

    a) _____

    b) _____

    c) _____

    d) _____

7) If I do Give IN, and drink while in possession of a vehicle, what will I do?

    a) _____

    b) _____

    c) _____

    d) _____

8) Instead of Drinking, what other things can I do to make me feel content?

    a) _____

    b) _____

    c) _____

    d) _____

Safety Plan Agreement

I am the (circle one) Significant Other, Family Member, or Support Member of person named below who has asked for my help to not drink and drive again.

_____ _____ .

This person named above is responsible for his/her own actions. This person has the ability to choose what to do and what not to do. As a support member, I agree to support and encourage this person in making the best positive choices.

I hereby agree to listen attentively to when _____ *comes to me with a problem related to alcohol or substance use. Please have both parties sign the agreement.*

Signed: _____ **Dated:** _____

Signed: _____ **Dated:** _____

Chapter 14

FINAL EXAM

Fill in the Blanks: Please no one word answers and be descriptive as possible.

1) Tom is driving down the road and he realizes one of his friends is at the local tavern, and this person owes Tom money. Tom decides to stop in and find this person as it is on the way home and he has other friends he could talk to as well. Tom is in what part of the Re-Arrest Chain,_____.

What should Tom have thought instead of pulling into the local tavern to keep himself safe? List at least 4 appropriate thoughts.

_____
_____
_____
_____
_____

2) Rick is driving down the road with Melody. He has always wanted to go out with her and she finally said yes. Rick is extremely nervous and feels a few drinks might loosen him up to be more sociable with Melody. At the tavern Rick orders his favorite drink and tells the bartender to make it stiff when Melody turns her head. What part of the Re-Arrest Chain is Rick in?_____.

What Thinking Errors is Rick using? List at least 4.

a)_____

b)_____

c)_____

d)_____

e)_____

What could Rick have done differently on this date?

_____
_____
_____
_____
_____

3) Mary just got into a huge argument with boyfriend and told him she never wanted to see him again. She left his apartment and slammed the door breaking the glass door on the way out as she was using profanity all the neighbors could hear. She realized she said very mean things that would end the relationship forever. What should Mary do? List at least 4 things she could do besides drink?

a)_____

b)_____

c)_____

d)_____

e)_____

4) List 5 benefits a person can expect from abstinence from alcohol?

a)_____

b)_____

c)_____

d)_____

e)_____

5) What is a Defense Mechanism?

_____
_____
_____

6) What are 4 cognitive or behavioral problems with children that have been exposed to alcohol or drug use during pregnancy?

a) _____

b) _____

c)_____

d)_____

7) Why does alcohol create Cirrhosis of the liver?

_____
_____
_____

8) What are some of the damaging effects on the brain from the use of alcohol in large quantities?

_____
_____
_____

9) What does Compartmentalizing mean?

_____
_____
_____

10) List 5 things you can use to help control drinking?

a) _____
_____

b) _____
_____

c) _____
_____

d _____
_____

11) List 3 reasons why a support system is important?

a) _____
_____
_____

b) _____
_____
_____

c) _____
_____
_____

12) List 3 Urge Control Skills.

a) _____
_____

b) _____
_____

c) _____
_____

13) What are the two most important words that help someone stop a D.U.I?

_____
_____

14) What is an Internal Boundary?

_____
_____
_____

Give an example of several Internal Boundaries.

_____
_____
_____

15) What is an External Boundary?

_____
_____
_____

16) Why is the D.U.I. Cycle important?

_____
_____
_____
_____
_____
_____

17) Why is the Relapse Prevention Plan important? (List several reasons)

_____

_____

_____

_____

_____

18) If you found yourself in a situation you felt you were being pressured to drink, what would you do to get out of it? (List 3 things)

_____

_____

_____

_____

_____

_____

19) If you found yourself intoxicated while in possession of your vehicle, what would you do to keep yourself from getting another D.U.I.? (List at Least 4 things)

_____

_____

_____

_____

_____

_____

_____

_____

_____

_____

_____

AUTOBIOGRAPHY

Mr. Phillip Karpinski presently lives in Las Vegas, Nevada. He graduated Cum Laude from the University of Delaware in 1995, with a Bachelor's Degree in Psychology and a Minor in Philosophy. He is a member the Psychology Honor Society and a member of the Philosophy Honor Society, which was achieved by academic excellence. Mr. Karpinski was accepted into a doctoral program for clinical psychology, but chose to go into the field of Clinical Social Work, where he received his Master's of Clinical Social Work from the University of Nevada, Las Vegas, in 1999. Mr. Karpinski completed his first internship of clinical social work in 1996, with Bridge Counseling, where he was co-facilitating substance abuse group counseling, and individual counseling. Mr. Karpinski is presently the co-owner of Evergreen Counseling in Las Vegas, and has been a therapist there for nine years. Mr. Karpinski has conducted over a thousand group counseling sessions for clients that present emotional or behavioral problems, and substance abuse problems. Mr. Karpinski has conducted over 10,000 hours of clinical counseling while working for Evergreen Counseling.

Mr. Karpinski's other achievements have included Private Pilot, teaching martial over a 25 year span, nationally ranked as a martial arts competitor, winner of numerous martial arts competitions, including the black belt division at the Las Vegas Karate Championships, nominated to a Martial Arts Hall of Fame, Founder of Modern Martial Arts in Las Vegas, former Jiu-Jitsu instructor for Frank Mir (UFC World Heavyweight Champion), professional billiard competitor, winner of a national team championship in billiards (BCA), and was World Ranked by the Professional Pool Players Association (1980-1981).